Psalms for Sojourners

Psalms for Sojourners

James Limburg

Fortress Press
Minneapolis

PSALMS FOR SOJOURNERS
Second Edition
Copyright © 2002 Augsburg Fortress. All rights reserved.
Except for brief quotations in critical articles or reviews, no
part of this book may be reproduced in any manner with-
out prior written permission from the publisher. Write:
Permissions, Augsburg Fortress, Box 1209, Minneapolis,
MN 55440.

Cover art: *Avenue, Tuscany,* by Josephine Trotter. Used by
permission of SuperStock, Inc.

Interior illustrations: Tanja Butler, *Icon: Visual Images for
Every Sunday,* copyright © 2000 Augsburg Fortress. Used
by permission.

Book design: Beth Wright

ISBN 0-8006-3466-7

The paper used in this publication meets the minimum
requirements of American National Standard for Information Sciences—Permanence of Paper for Printed Library
Materials, ANSI Z329.48-1984.

Manufactured in the U.S.A.   AF 1-3466
06   05   04   03   02   1   2   3   4   5   6   7   8   9   10

In memory of my father
Stanley W. Limburg

Contents

Preface to the Second Edition   ix

Preface to the First Edition   xi

1. The Strength, the Passion, and
   the Fire: An Invitation to the Psalms   1
   The Strength, the Passion, and the Fire / 1
   R.S.V.P. (Psalm 1) / 5
   Messiah (Psalm 2) / 10
   The Book of Praises / 15

2. When the Bottom Drops Out:
   The Laments   21
   Asking the Hard Questions (Psalm 13) / 22
   When the Bottom Drops Out
      (Psalm 130) / 26
   "And Not So Hot on Why" (Psalm 22) / 34
   Praise and Lament in the Psalms / 38

3. The Way through the Darkness:
   Psalms of Trust   43
   Rock-a-bye Baby (Psalm 131) / 43
   The Way through the Darkness
      (Psalm 23) / 47
   The Hardest Part Comes Last
      (Psalm 71) / 53

When Good Things Happen to Bad People
(Psalm 73) / 59
The Trumpet Every Morning (Psalm 46) / 64

4. **Psalms for Sojourners: The Pilgrimage
Psalms**   69
A Psalm for Sojourners (Psalm 121) / 70
A Word for Worriers and Workaholics
(Psalm 127) / 74
Where It All Comes Together
(Psalm 133) / 79
The Pilgrimage Psalms / 83

5. **From King David to Duke Ellington:
The Hymns**   87
Sunrise, Sunset (Psalm 113) / 88
Time to Remember (Psalm 103) / 93
From King David to Duke Ellington
(Psalm 150) / 97
The Response of Praise / 101

6. **The World Is So Full of a Number
of Things: Creation Psalms**   105
Midway between the Apes and the Angels
(Psalm 8) / 106
The World Is So Full of a Number of Things
(Psalm 104) / 113
On Not Trying to Be Moses
(Psalm 139) / 118

For Further Reading   123

Acknowledgments   127

Preface to the Second Edition

I write these words on an October day in 2001. Just a few weeks ago, on September 11, life in our nation and in our twenty-first-century world was changed. Terrorists hijacked four airliners filled with passengers, crashing two of them into the twin towers of the World Trade Center in New York City and one into the Pentagon in Washington, D.C. Thousands were killed or injured. On the evening of that September day, President George W. Bush spoke briefly to the American people. Toward the end of his remarks he chose to quote Psalm 23: "Even though I walk through the valley of the shadow of death, I fear no evil, for you are with me." In our public as well as our private lives, these ancient psalms continue to express and address our deepest concerns.

In this new edition of *Psalms for Sojourners,* the New Revised Standard Version of the Bible has mainly replaced the older Revised Standard Version for the sake of clarity. A few changes have been made to the text of the book itself. The bibliography at the end of the book has been updated and expanded. Readers wishing to pursue the study of the Psalms in more depth can make use of the resources listed there, including my own recently published commentary on the Psalms.

It continues to be my hope that these reflections will increase your appreciation and understanding of these psalms as they accompany you through the joys and the sorrows of your own sojourn.

Preface to the First Edition

Sojourner. The word has an old-fashioned, biblical ring. It means, according to my dictionary, one who lives in a place temporarily, as on a visit. The word has this sense in the Bible. Abraham described himself as "a stranger and a sojourner" when he was living temporarily in Hittite territory (Gen. 23:4 RSV). Moses said of his time spent in Midian, "I have been a sojourner in a foreign land" (Exod. 2:22 RSV).

Sojourner. The word has yet another sense in the Bible. It can be used for the totality of a person's earthly existence, picturing the whole of life as a journey or a sojourn. The aged Jacob says to the ruler of Egypt, "The days of the years of my sojourning are a hundred and thirty years" (Gen. 47:9 RSV). Or the psalmist says to God, "For I am thy passing guest, a sojourner, like all my fathers" (Ps. 39:12 RSV).

It is with this second sense that the word is used in the title of this book. The idea came from a study of Psalm 121. That psalm originated as a psalm for travelers, declaring the Lord's protection for them as they set out on a pilgrimage to

Jerusalem. Psalm 121 has been used as a traveler's psalm ever since, appropriate for the time at the beginning of a journey. But a careful reading indicates that the psalm also speaks a more comprehensive word, one that embraces the whole of life's journey. "The LORD will . . . keep your life. The LORD will keep your going out and your coming in from this time on and forevermore," it concludes (vv. 7-8).

Consideration of that psalm for sojourners invites a careful listening to the other pilgrimage psalms of which it is a part (Chapter 4) and then to other psalms as well. In giving them a hearing, we discover that they, too, have a way of moving from a particular situation to a more general application. They address the days of our own lives, in times of hurting as well as times of happiness, helping us to learn how to pray and also how to praise.

After the introduction in the first part of Chapter 1, this book consists of reflections on psalms of various types, with an eye toward their meaning for contemporary life. Comments have been made along the way to direct the reader who wishes to descend more deeply into the depths of the psalms. The book concludes with a list of readings that I have found to be especially valuable.

The purpose of the book may be described as incendiary. It is my hope that these reflections on selected psalms will ignite your interest in this ancient hymnbook and prayer book, and that you will be warmed, fired, and inspired by them as they accompany you on your sojourn.

I wish to acknowledge my indebtedness to two teachers who have helped me to understand the Psalms. Professor Gerhard Frost first introduced me to the Psalms in an academic setting in a college religion course. More recently, the lectures and writings of Professor Claus Westermann have been immensely illuminating; those familiar with Old Testament scholarship will quickly recognize my indebtedness to him.

As I was at my desk finishing this manuscript, I received a call notifying me of the sudden death of my father. He loved the Psalms, particularly in their Dutch musical settings. It seems appropriate to dedicate this to his memory.

chapter 1

The Strength, the Passion, and the Fire: An Invitation to the Psalms

The Strength, the Passion, and the Fire

My first introduction to the study of the Psalms took place long ago in a Sunday school class in the basement of a church in Minnesota. The teacher was a small woman with dark hair and a bright smile, the mother of one of my best friends. She handed out a stack of worn, black King James Versions. "Now take your Bible," she said, "and open it right to the middle. There you will find the Psalms."

Since that time I often have quoted her instructions as I've taught the Psalms in settings ranging from mountain retreats and lakeshores to classrooms, convents, and even the basement of a city hall, where a group of policemen were working on a college degree.

I think it fitting that the Psalms are located in the middle of the Bible, between accounts of holy wars and conquests on the one side and the good news on the other. That is because, in the years since first being introduced to them, I have encountered the Psalms in the middle of life, giving expression both to the sorrows and the joys that mark our days.

One December morning, for instance, a half dozen of us walked through the mist and fog at Dachau, the concentration camp where thousands of Jews and political prisoners died. As we made our way to the crematorium, I remembered author Elie Wiesel telling about the gentle Hasidic Jews of Eastern Europe, old people and children, walking toward the gas chambers and singing the Hebrew Psalms as they went. I stepped into a memorial chapel and saw the words of Psalm 130 on the wall, "*aus der tiefe rufe ich, herr, zu dir,*" and I could imagine hundreds, thousands, millions of prayers ascending to heaven: "Out of the depths I cry to you, O Lord."

The Psalms reflect the good times, too. An aged widow, living alone in a small Midwestern town, was telling me about her children. "Then there was Lambert," she said, "but of course he's gone now. He always said the horses plowed best for him because he sang the Psalms to them in Dutch." Think of the ingredients in that scene: psalms that originated in Hebrew in Israel, sung in Dutch by the grandson of an immigrant from the Netherlands, as he plowed with horses on a prairie in America.

Another scene: One summer I was teaching the Psalms to campers in the Black Hills of South Dakota. They all learned to sing a Hebrew song based on the first line of Psalm 133. Translated, the words mean, "How very good and pleasant it is when God's people live together in unity." Several years later I received a postcard from one of those campers, at that time a counselor at a camp in the state of New York. "I thought you'd like to know," he began, "that I taught my campers that Hebrew song. We were hiking through the woods singing it when we ran into another group of hikers who heard us and joined right in! They were Jewish kids from New York City. That psalm brought us together." How good and pleasant indeed, I thought, when Christians and Jews meet out in the woods and join together in singing a psalm.

These prayers and hymns, found in the middle of the Bible, have a way of turning up in the middle of our lives. The book *Occasional Services: A Companion to Lutheran Book of Worship* (Minneapolis: Augsburg, 1982) assigns psalms to a variety of life's situations: sickness and gratitude, childbirth and stillbirth, loneliness, and the blessing of a dwelling. That the Psalms should be invited to such occasions is not surprising, since they originated in similar situations. They come from the depths of sorrow (130) or the heights of celebration (150). They reflect the pain of loneliness (42) and the joy of community (133). They allow us to hear the prayer of an old person worried about what lies ahead (71) or to look in on the everyday life of a young family happily gathered around their table (128).

The Psalms in the middle of our Bibles originated in the midst of life and continue to speak to us, and *for* us, in the midst of our lives. Dietrich Bonhoeffer, who loved the Psalms, quoted Luther: "Whoever has begun to pray the Psalter seriously and regularly will soon give a vacation to other little devotional prayers and say: 'Ah, there is not the juice, the strength, the passion, the fire, which I find in the Psalter'" (*Psalms: The Prayer Book of the Bible* [Minneapolis: Augsburg, 1970], 25).

The pages that follow are offered as an invitation to the Psalms. We begin with Psalms 1 and 2, which have been placed at the beginning of the book of Psalms as an introduction, and continue by considering five groups of psalms: laments, psalms of trust, pilgrimage psalms, hymns, and creation psalms. My hope is that through this exploration of the Psalms you will discover for yourself what Luther found in them: "the juice, the strength, the passion, and the fire."

* * *

Happy are those
    who reject the advice of evil men,
who do not follow the example of sinners

or join those who have no use for God.
Instead, they find joy in obeying the Law of
    the LORD,
    and they study it day and night.
They are like trees that grow beside a
    stream,
    that bear fruit at the right time,
    and whose leaves do not dry up.
They succeed in everything they do.

But evil men are not like this at all;
    they are like straw that the wind blows
        away.
Sinners will be condemned by God
    and kept apart from God's own people.
The righteous are guided and protected by
    the LORD,
    but the evil are on the way to their doom.
                                —Psalm 1 (TEV)

R.S.V.P. (Psalm 1)

The professor of philosophy was telling us how
he had learned to play the piano.

"At the beginning," he said, "my folks couldn't
get me to practice. My mother made a chart and
asked me to mark it each day. I didn't do it. They
promised me a dollar a week if I'd put in a half
hour each day. That didn't do it either. Finally,
they resorted to threats: 'Practice, or else . . . ,'
they said. But I still didn't practice.

"Then I got a new teacher. At my first lesson, she told me to sit down in a chair and listen. She sat at the piano and played Beethoven's *Moonlight Sonata.* I had never heard it before, and I was hooked. I wanted more than anything to be able to make music like that. She had given me a vision of the kind of piano player I could be. With the melodies of Beethoven running through my head, I went home and started practicing scales and arpeggios, and I've kept on playing ever since."

This psalm is an invitation to a lifetime of living with the themes and the melodies of the Bible. There are no suggestions of weekly or daily quotas. There are no dos and don'ts, no threats. But there is a picture of the person who makes a practice of listening to what Scripture says. Such persons are

> . . . like trees that grow beside a stream,
>   that bear fruit at the right time,
>   and whose leaves do not dry up.
> They succeed in everything they do. (v. 3)

This psalm was placed at the beginning of the book of Psalms for a reason. It is an invitation to a way of life described as "blessed," that is, happy. That way is first described negatively:

> Happy are those
>   who reject the advice of evil men,
> who do not follow the example of sinners

or join those who have no use for God.
(v. 1 TEV)

Then the way is described positively:

but their delight is in the law of the LORD,
and on his law they meditate day and
night. (v. 2)

The word *law* calls for some explanation. In the Hebrew original, the word is *torah,* which means "instruction" or "teaching." *Torah* came to mean the collected instructions or teachings of the Lord, and thus is close to what we mean when we speak of Scripture or the Bible. The person who is like that tree, deeply rooted and growing, is the one who reads, hears, and reflects on the Lord's teachings as found in the Bible.

The first psalm introduces the book of Psalms not only as a hymnbook, but also as a prayer book. It is an invitation to day-by-day listening to the themes and the melodies of Scripture and in so doing to find inspiration, comfort, and direction.

Dietrich Bonhoeffer was a German pastor killed by the Nazis at the end of World War II. In letters he wrote from prison, he spoke to friends about the "secret discipline." By this he meant the daily practice of reading a portion of the Bible, thinking about it, and praying. Bonhoeffer was very much involved in the political events of the war, even to the extent of participating in a plot on Hitler's life. But along with this deep political involvement went a deep commitment to the secret discipline. Bonhoeffer's idea of the relationship between the two has been summarized: "The secret discipline without worldly involvement ends up in a ghetto; worldly involvement without the secret discipline is just so much noise and a sham" (Eberhard Bethge, *Dietrich Bonhoeffer* [Munich: Kaiser, 1967], 992; my translation).

This psalm is an invitation to the daily discipline of reading the Bible, reflecting on it, and praying.

Once my wife and I were guests of a couple who lived in a village in northern Germany. He had been a farmer, she a teacher. Now they were retired. As we stepped into their home, I noticed a poem by Bonhoeffer hanging on the wall. Our meal began with prayer. After the meal, our host tore a page from a devotional calendar and read a portion of Scripture with a short explanation. Our conversation turned to the difficulties of the war years and the challenges of this time of peace.

As we left their home, I thought about the importance of that tradition of family devotions, of daily living with the themes and the melodies of the Bible, and of that picture of a tree solidly rooted beside a flowing stream.

This psalm is an invitation to a lifetime of day-by-day Bible reading, reflection, and prayer. This invitation is marked with an R.S.V.P.—respond, if you please.

The Wisdom Psalms

The first psalm in the Psalter is a *wisdom psalm.* While the mood of most psalms is either hot with praise or cold with complaint, the tone of the wisdom psalms is more cool and reflective. Other wisdom psalms are 127, 128, and 133, which are collections of short sayings, and 37, 49, and 112.

The central theme of the first psalm is meditation on Torah or Scripture as the pathway to a happy and blessed life. One other psalm has this same theme: Psalm 119, the longest of the psalms. Psalm 119 speaks of the word of God as "a lamp to my feet and a light to my path" (v. 105) and commends meditation on the written word (vv. 15, 23, 48, 97, 99, 148). Since Psalms 120–134 existed as a separate collection (see Chapter 4), it seems likely that an earlier edition of the book of Psalms consisted of Psalm 1–119, these two Torah-psalms forming bookends for the collection as a whole.

* * *

Why do the nations plan rebellion?
Why do people make their useless plots?
Their kings revolt,
    their rulers plot together against the LORD
    and against the king he chose.
"Let us free ourselves from their rule," they
    say;
    "let us throw off their control."

From his throne in heaven the LORD laughs
   and mocks their feeble plans.
Then he warns them in anger
   and terrifies them with his fury.
"On Zion, my sacred hill," he says,
   "I have installed my king."

"I will announce," says the king,
"what the LORD has declared.
   He said to me: 'You are my son;
   today I have become your father.
Ask, and I will give you all the nations;
   the whole earth will be yours.
You will break them with an iron rod;
   you will shatter them in pieces like a clay
      pot.'"
Now listen to this warning, you kings;
   learn this lesson, you rulers of the world:
Serve the LORD with fear;
   tremble and bow down to him;
or else his anger will be quickly aroused,
   and you will suddenly die.
Happy are all who go to him for protection.
                              —Psalm 2 (TEV)

Messiah (Psalm 2)

When I was growing up, my favorite time of the
year was the period between Thanksgiving and
Christmas. This was the time of the first snow-
fall, the freezing of the river, and hockey each

night after school. Downtown, the streetlights were decorated with green wreaths. Christmas trees appeared in the corridors at school. On the day before vacation, grades 1–8 gathered at an intersection in the hallway to sing carols. I can still hear the countermelody on the second stanza of "Oh, Come, All Ye Faithful," sung by the junior high chorus. It began, "Sing, choirs of angels," and then these words were seconded by a stratospheric soprano line, "Sing, choirs of angels. . . ."

There was also the Christmas program at church. Our turn came to put on bathrobes, twist towels around our heads, and walk down the aisle carrying long canes wrapped with white adhesive tape. Two friends and I stood there, shepherds for that night, alongside three boys crowned as wise men and a trio of angelic girls wearing white wings that were stored back of the furnace the rest of the year. Afterward came the reward: a brown sack filled with peanuts, hard candy, and an apple as red as the cheeks of the hatchery owner whose annual task it was to hand them out to us.

College added a new dimension to this favorite time of the year: Handel's *Messiah*. An enthusiastic director rounded up half the student body and a few faculty for rehearsals in a basement practice room. Such music I had never heard before. We left the practice room one night with "For unto us a child is born" running through our heads and stepped outside to discover a scene of unforgettable beauty: huge white snowflakes were gently falling in the darkness of the winter night. Since that time, the *Messiah* has always been a part of our Advent season.

The *Messiah*. The word means "anointed one." In the Old Testament it came to mean the long-awaited one who would be a king like David. These hopes for a coming Messiah had their beginnings in psalms originally composed for events in the life of the king (2, 45, 72, 110).

Psalm 2 was written for the inauguration of a new king. At such occasions, rulers of nations subject to Jerusalem would be on hand. They would be wondering, "What will this new king be like? Is this the moment to rebel and make our declaration of independence?" Psalm 2 reflects this situation:

> Why do the nations plan rebellion?
> Why do the people make their useless
>   plots? . . .
> Their rulers plot together against the LORD
>   and against the king he chose.
> "Let us free ourselves from their rule," they
>   say. (v. 1-3 TEV)

Then the psalm tells of the Lord's reaction to all of this:

> From his throne in heaven the LORD laughs
>   and mocks their feeble plans. (v. 4 TEV)

The king reports what the Lord has said to him:

> He said to me: "You are my son;
> today I have become your father.
> Ask, and I will give you all the nations;
>   the whole earth will be yours."
> (vv. 7-8 TEV)

As time went on, these psalms laid extravagant hopes on the shoulders of each new king. May he rule forever over the whole earth, with justice, righteousness, and peace (72:2, 5, 7, 8)! The king was even called God's son (2:7). He was to have special concern for the poor and needy (72:4, 12-14).

But king after king was a disappointment. David became involved in a tawdry affair with a soldier's wife and then in a murder plot. Solomon's wealth and his wives went to his head. An innocent citizen was killed because Ahab wanted his property for a vegetable garden. And so on.

Jerusalem was destroyed by the Babylonians, and the time of the kings was ended. But the hope for a great king, a Messiah, lived on. They had been expanded and fine-tuned by the prophets and were treasured by the people.

Then came a surprise. Back of a Bethlehem inn, a young woman gave birth to a child. On hand were a few shepherds, some wise men, and a company of angels. Did they carry long canes and wear crowns? Were the angels powered by white wings? The texts don't say.

But one thing is certain. There was singing. Luke reports the words the angels sang:

> Glory to God in the highest heaven,
> and on earth peace among those
>   whom he favors! (Luke 2:14)

What was the tune? We'd like to know. I'm guessing they used Handel.

The Seedbed for Messianic Hope

Psalm 2 is one of a group called the *royal psalms.* These were originally composed for events in the life of the king, such as a wedding (45), a coronation or the anniversary of one (2, 72, 101, 110), preparation before a battle (20, 144:1-11), celebration of a victory (18, 21), or the affirmation of the Lord's choice of David as king and Mount Zion as the place for worship (89, 132).

These royal psalms speak of the king in the most grandiose terms. He is called God's son (2:7), God's firstborn (89:27), or God's anointed, which in Hebrew is *messiah* (2:2; 18:50; 20:6). The king is invited to take the place of honor at the Lord's right hand (110:1). His rule will be over all nations (2:8-12; 18:44-45; 72:8-11), and the hope is expressed that he will rule forever (72:5). His administration will be marked by justice, righteousness, and peace (72:2, 5-8) and by a special concern for the poor and weak (72:4, 12-14).

As the story of the monarchy unfolded in history, king after king failed to measure up to these grand expectations. In 587 B.C.E., the monarchy came to an end with the destruction of Jerusalem. These hopes for a great king or anointed one or messiah were picked up by the prophets and projected into the future. In this way the royal psalms became the seedbed for messianic hope.

The Book of Praises

Martin Luther introduced his German translation of the Psalms with these words:

> [The Psalter] might well be called a little Bible. In it is comprehended most beautifully and briefly everything that is in the entire Bible. It is really a fine enchiridion or handbook. In fact, I have a notion that the Holy Spirit wanted to take the trouble himself to compile a short Bible and book of examples of all Christendom or all saints, so that anyone who could not read the whole Bible would here have anyway almost an entire summary of it, comprised in one little book. (*Luther's Works*, vol. 35 [Philadelphia: Fortress, 1960], 254)

The Psalms can be approached in a variety of ways. One can read and reflect on one psalm on its own; think of the countless times the comforting words of Psalm 23 have been heard in this way. Or, a psalm can be considered in the context of other psalms of the same type; one royal psalm, for example, could be studied in conjunction with the others in that group (see "The Seedbed…" above). Or the Laments could be considered together (see Chapter 2), or the Hymns (see Chapter 5). Now, at the beginning of the twenty-first century, the emphasis is on reading each psalm in its literary context, whether that be the context of neighboring psalms (Psalms 103–104 or 130–131), or the context of a collection (Psalms 120–134), or the context of the entire book of Psalms, called the Psalter. James Mays, whose commentary illustrates this approach, has called this method of reading psalms "going by the book." Luther was thinking of the Psalms in this way in the quotation above. I offer here some observations about the book of Psalms as a whole.

Going by the Book
The first words of a speech, the first notes of a symphony, or the first lines of a book are all crafted with great care. The author or composer knows that the introduction will set the tone for the whole work. Psalms 1 and 2 are a double introduction to the book of Psalms. The editor of the Psalter has linked them together. Unlike the

psalms that follow, they have no titles; they are framed with sayings that began, "Happy are. . ." (1:1; 2:12).

We have seen that Psalm 1 introduces the entire Psalter as a book designed to be a basis for meditation and a help for prayer. Again, a quotation from Luther about the whole book of Psalms: "As a teacher will compose letters or little speeches for his pupils to write to their parents, so by this book He [God's Spirit] prepares both the language and the mood in which we should address the Heavenly Father and pray for that which the other books have taught us to do and to imitate" (*Luther's Works,* vol. 14 [St. Louis: Concordia, 1958], 286).

Psalm 2 suggests that an important theme in the psalms that will follow is the anointed one, or Messiah. It is a signal to watch for this theme in other psalms. The editor has scattered the royal psalms throughout the Psalter; two are placed at particularly strategic points, the conclusion of Book II (72) and of Book III (89). Psalm 2 thus directs the reader to listen for what the Psalms have to say about the Messiah.

The Five Books
The Psalter in its present form has been divided into five "books." Jewish tradition suggests that this five-part division corresponds to the five parts at the beginning of the Old Testament:

"Moses gave Israel the five books, and David gave Israel the five books of psalms." Each of these books ends on a note of praise:

> Praise the LORD, the God of Israel!
> Praise him now and forever!
>   (Book I, 41:13 TEV)

> Praise his glorious name forever!
>   May his glory fill the whole world.
> Amen! Amen! (Book II, 72:19 TEV)

> Praise the LORD forever!
> Amen! Amen! (Book III, 89:52 TEV)

> Praise the LORD, the God of Israel;
>   praise him now and forever!
>   (Book IV, 106:48 TEV)

> Praise the LORD.... (150:1, plus all of Psalm
>   150, which concludes Book V and the
>   entire Psalter)

From Lament to Praise

The book of Psalms as a whole moves from lament to praise. After the introductory pair, the psalms in the first part of the Psalter are cries for help from the times of trouble (3; 4; 5; 6; 7; 11; 12; 13; 14; 16; 17; and so forth). The Psalter concludes with a quintet of psalms of praise, each beginning and ending with "Praise the Lord" or, in Hebrew, *Hallelujah* (146–150).

The German theologian Ludwig Koehler once wrote, "The deeper one descends through the centuries into the breadth of the Old Testament writings, the louder the praise and laud of God can be heard" (quoted by Westermann in *Praise and Lament* [see "For Further Reading"], 7). The Hebrew title for the Psalter catches its contents in one word: *Tehillim,* that is, "praises." The book of Psalms is, at bottom, a book of praises.

chapter 2

When the Bottom Drops Out: The Laments

How much longer will you forget me, LORD?
   Forever?
How much longer will you hide yourself
   from me?
How long must I endure trouble?
How long will sorrow fill my heart day and
   night?
How long will my enemies triumph over me?

Look at me, O LORD my God, and answer
   me.
   Restore my strength; don't let me die.
Don't let my enemies say, "We have defeated
   him."
   Don't let them gloat over my downfall.

I rely on your constant love;
   I will be glad, because you will rescue me.
I will sing to you, O LORD,
   because you have been good to me.
                    —Psalm 13 (TEV)

Asking the Hard Questions (Psalm 13)`

We sat at the small kitchen table where we had visited many times before. He was in his seventies, retired, with a zest for life and a sense of humor that ordinarily punctuated our conversations with wit and laughter. But that night he had just returned from visiting his wife in the hospital, and the news was not good. She had been battling cancer for years. Now she was entering into one of her periodic bouts of depression. She would have to be moved to the psychiatric floor.

Even though I'd known him for several months, we had never discussed theological issues before. That night we did. "You're a pastor," he said; "now you tell me: Why is God doing this to her? She has always been good to everybody. She doesn't deserve it. Why is God doing this? Why?"

When I walked home that night, those questions were ringing in my ears: Why? Why? Why? Such questions, of course, are the hardest ones that we humans ever ask. Jesus asked such a question on the cross. In the most difficult time of his life, he made a question from Psalm 22 his own question, "My God, my God, why have you forsaken me?" (Matt. 27:46). In praying this ancient prayer, Jesus pointed us to the Psalms for those times when we too ask, "Why, Lord?" or "How long?"

More specifically, Jesus points us to the psalms that arise from times of trouble, the *laments*.

Psalm 13 is a good introduction to the laments because it contains all of the elements typical of these psalms. It begins with a *complaint*, in the form of a series of questions:

> How much longer will you forget me LORD? . . .
> How much longer must I endure trouble? . . .
> How long will my enemies triumph over me? (vv. 1-2 TEV)

Claus Westermann has called attention to the three dimensions of the complaint in this psalm and in all the laments. The first is a *you-complaint*, directed toward God. Next is an *I-complaint*, centered on the person praying. The final question is a *they-complaint*, focused on other people. These psalms of lament express the fullness of human suffering. These are the words of a person who has no peace with God, self, or others. They reveal the theological, psychological, and sociological dimensions of suffering.

After the complaint in Psalm 13 we hear the *request*. The one praying asks something of God, and the requests correspond to the three dimensions of the complaint. God, says the psalmist, has not been paying attention: the request is, "Look at me, O Lord God, and answer me." The I-complaint spoke of the individual's pain; the request is, "Restore my strength; don't let me die." The last complaint was about other people;

the request is, "Don't let [my enemies] gloat over my downfall" (vv. 3-4 TEV).

A third element in the psalms of lament is the affirmation of *trust*. This psalm continues, "I rely on your constant love; I will be glad, because you will rescue me" (v. 5 TEV).

Finally, the psalms of lament almost always include an element of *praise*. Psalm 13 concludes with, "I will sing to you, O LORD, because you have been good to me" (v. 6 TEV).

These are the elements that make up the psalms of lament in our Bible: *complaint, request, trust, praise*. If you begin reading through the book of Psalms, you can discover the laments with these elements. But how can these psalms help us with our own hard questions? How can they help us with the "Whys" and the "How longs" that arise from the sickrooms, the cemeteries, the conversations across kitchen tables in our own lives?

First of all, as we read through these psalms, we discover that these hard questions are not directed to friends or even to priests or theologians. They are addressed to God: "I am worn out, O LORD; have pity on me! . . . How long, O LORD, will you wait to help me?" (Ps. 6:2-3 TEV). "My God, my God, why have you abandoned me?" (Ps. 22:1 TEV). "How much longer, LORD, will you just look on?" (Ps. 35:17 TEV). These psalms don't suppress the "Whys" or "How longs," as if the questions were impolite or irreverent. They encourage us to do as Jesus did, to address our hard questions to God.

Second, as we listen to these questions in the Psalms, we discover something quite astonishing: The questions are never answered. Never is a "How long?" answered with "Yet three more weeks. . . ." Never is a "Why?" answered with "Because. . . ." The questions remain questions. Even Jesus did not get an answer to the "Why?" that he cried out from the cross. Some of our questions, it appears, will have to remain questions. The answers are hidden with God.

Finally, these psalms never end with the questions. They also include requests, affirmations of trust, and, in almost every case, words of praise. The questions do remain questions. But somehow the one who raises them can go on with life and can even join the company of believers in praising God.

There are times when it hurts too much even to pray. In such situations maybe the only prayer can be an agonized "Why?" At such times, you should remember that you are not the first to ask such a question. Others have been there, too. You can find their questions and prayers recorded in the Psalms. It may be that these psalms of lament can help you to move from complaint and request to trust, and even, once again, to praise.

* * *

Out of the depths I cry to you, O LORD.
  Lord, hear my voice!
Let your ears be attentive
  to the voice of my supplications!

If you, O LORD, should mark iniquities,
  Lord, who could stand?
But there is forgiveness with you,
  so that you may be revered.
I wait for the LORD, my soul waits,
  and in his word I hope;
my soul waits for the LORD
    more than those who watch for the
      morning,
    more than those who watch for the
      morning.

O Israel, hope in the LORD!
  For with the LORD there is steadfast love,
  and with him is great power to redeem.
It is he who will redeem Israel
  from all its iniquities.
                              —Psalm 130

When the Bottom Drops Out (Psalm 130)

There are words that hit you like a blow, sending you reeling, plummeting into the depths. They may be spoken in the quiet of an evening, from one college sophomore to another: "I'm sorry. I just don't love you anymore." They may come across the desk of a plant supervisor: "You've done a great job for us, but now we're going to have to do some downsizing. Your position will have to be eliminated." They may be heard in the antiseptic sterility of a doctor's office. "We have the results from the lab. I'm afraid it's cancer." Or in the waiting room of a hospital: "Your wife is fine. But the baby didn't make it."

Once those words have been spoken, everything changes. The rest of the world goes on as usual, but your world will never be the same. All of the supports are gone. The bottom has dropped out. You feel yourself sinking into the depths.

Psalm 130 comes out of such a situation. Because it is a prayer, a cry that emerges from the depths, it can help us in such situations. The Lutheran church has recognized this and has assigned this psalm to the most difficult times in life: stillbirth, death shortly after birth, burial (*Occasional Services: A Companion to Lutheran Book of Worship* [Minneapolis: Augsburg, 1982], 55, 109). Those who built the memorial chapel at the Dachau concentration camp knew the power of this psalm. They put the first five verses on the wall there, beginning with the cry from the depths and ending with an expression of hope.

One of the pilgrimage psalms (see Chapter 4) intended for the journey to Jerusalem, this psalm is important for the journeys of our own lives. Since Jerusalem lies in the mountains, traveling there meant ascending the heights and descending into the valleys. Life's journey has its hills and valleys, too. Some psalms are suited for the highs, the mountaintop experiences. This one is designed for the lows, the valleys, the depths.

We recognize some of the characteristic marks of the lament. At the beginning is a *request*, "Lord, hear me!" Behind that request is an implied *complaint*, "I'm about to go under, Lord, and you aren't paying any attention!"

> Out of the depths I cry to you, O LORD.
>> LORD, hear my voice!
> Let your ears be attentive
>> to the voice of my supplications! (vv. 1-2)

The person crying for help pictures himself as drowning, in deep water. The same imagery appears in Ps. 69:1-2:

> Save me, O God,
>> for the waters have come up to my neck.
> I sink in deep mire,
>> where there is no foothold;
> I have come into deep waters,
>> and the flood sweeps over me.

The problem of the one who cries out is not just one of physical pain. Nor is it only an emotional problem, a depression. It is not only a spiritual problem, that of being weighted down with sin. The person crying out does not "have" a problem at all. At issue is survival. In this psalm, it is a matter of life—or death.

Then the tone of the psalm begins to change. The person praying looks inward and sees a failure: "If you, O LORD, should mark iniquities, Lord, who could stand?" The psalmist looks at God and sees that "there is forgiveness with you."

Now the "I cry" changes to a "I wait" and "I hope." The image is of a watchman who is weary after staying at his post through the long hours of the night. How that watchman longs for the first rays of the morning sun!

> I wait for the LORD, my soul waits,
>   and in his word I hope:
> my soul waits for the LORD
>   more than those who watch for the
>   morning,
>   more than those who watch for the
>   morning.

How could the "I cry" of the person about to go under be transformed into the "I hope" of one who expects to be rescued? The affirmation of *trust* in v. 7 provides the clue: "For with the LORD there is steadfast love, and with him is great power to redeem."

This "steadfast love" is the kind of love that keeps on loving, no matter what. The same Hebrew word is used for the love that young Hosea had for his wife, even when he discovered that she was being unfaithful to him (Hosea 1–3). This is the kind of love that never gives up, like that of the father who never gave up on his rebellious son and kept hoping, waiting, watching for his return (Luke 15). Because of this love that will not let go, the "I cry" of the one about to go under is finally stilled and is transformed into an affirmation of trust in the Lord who will come to the rescue (v. 7).

The psalm concludes with a word for all who hear it: "Hope in the LORD. . . . He will rescue you from all your sins" (v. 8, paraphrased).

Luther called this a "Pauline psalm" because it speaks so clearly about sin and forgiveness. It is also Pauline because it knows of the heights and the depths of human existence. The apostle knew what it was to be in the depths: "Three times I was shipwrecked; for a night and a day I was adrift at sea," he wrote (2 Cor. 11:25). Paul also knew something about that steadfast love of God: "For I am convinced that neither death, nor life, nor angels, nor rulers, nor things present, nor things to come, nor powers, nor height, nor depth, nor anything else in all creation, will be able to separate us from the love of God in Christ Jesus our Lord" (Rom. 8:38–39).

"Nor height, nor depth," said the apostle. The good news is this: No matter how deep you've gotten in over your head, no matter how low your life has sunk, no matter how badly you've gotten bogged down in the muck and the mire, you are never out of the range of God's love.

Our cries from the depths, says this psalm, can be stilled and transformed into waiting and hoping. Notice that Psalms 130 and 131 are linked, with the same call for hope in 130:7a and 131:3a. In this way, the anguished prayer for help in 130 is tied to the expression of trust and hope in 131.

* * *

My God, my God, why have you aban-
　　doned me?
I have cried desperately for help,
　　but still it does not come.
During the day I call to you, my God,
　　but you do not answer;
I call at night,
　　but get no rest.
But you are enthroned as the Holy One,
　　the one whom Israel praises.
Our ancestors put their trust in you;
　　they trusted you, and you saved them.
They called to you and escaped from danger;
　　they trusted you and were not disappointed.

But I am no longer a man; I am a worm,
　　despised and scorned by everyone!
All who see me make fun of me;
　　they stick out their tongues and shake
　　　　their heads.

"You relied on the LORD," they say.
　"Why doesn't he save you?
If the LORD likes you,
　why doesn't he help you?"

It was you who brought me safely through
　　birth,
　and when I was a baby, you kept me safe.
I have relied on you since the day I was
　　born,
　and you have always been my God.
Do not stay away from me!
　Trouble is near,
　and there is no one to help.

Many enemies surround me like bulls;
　they are all around me,
　like fierce bulls from the land of Bashan.
They open their mouths like lions,
　roaring and tearing at me.

My strength is gone,
　gone like water spilled on the ground.
All my bones are out of joint;
　my heart is like melted wax.
My throat is as dry as dust,
　and my tongue sticks to the roof of my
　　　mouth.
You have left me for dead in the dust.

A gang of evil men is around me;
    like a pack of dogs they close in on me;
    they tear at my hands and feet.
All my bones can be seen.
    My enemies look at me and stare.
They gamble for my clothes
    and divide them among themselves.

O Lord, don't stay away from me!
    Come quickly to my rescue!
Save me from the sword;
    save my life from these dogs.
Rescue me from these lions;
    I am helpless before these wild bulls.

I will tell my people what you have done;
    I will praise you in their assembly;
"Praise him, you servants of the Lord!
    Honor him, you descendants of Jacob!
    Worship him, you people of Israel!
He does not neglect the poor or ignore their
        suffering;
    he does not turn away from them,
    but answers when they call for help."

In the full assembly I will praise you
    for what you have done;
    in the presence of those who worship you
    I will offer the sacrifices I promised.
The poor will eat as much as they want;

those who come to the LORD will praise
him.
May they prosper forever!

All nations will remember the LORD.
From every part of the world they will
turn to him;
all races will worship him.
The LORD is king,
and he rules the nations.

All proud men will bow down to him,
all mortal men will bow down before him.
Future generations will serve him;
men will speak of the LORD to the coming
generation.
People not yet born will be told:
"The LORD saved his people."

—Psalm 22 (TEV)

"And Not So Hot on Why" (Psalm 22)

The hardest questions are those that begin with
"Why?" "Why does she have to suffer?" "Why
doesn't God do something?" "Why me?"

The hardest question Jesus raised began with
"Why?" One of the "seven last words" from the
cross, it is the only one of these sayings remembered in Hebrew, and the only one that is a
question: *Eli, Eli, lema sabachthani?* That is,

"My God, my God, why have you forsaken me?" (Matt. 27:46).

The rock opera *Jesus Christ Superstar* imagines that Jesus asked such questions even before Good Friday. In the Garden of Gethsemane, Jesus is speaking to God:

> Can you show me now that I would not be killed in vain?
> Show me just a little of your omnipresent brain.
> Show me there's a reason for your wanting me to die.
> You're far too keen on where and how,
> and not so hot on why.

If Jesus felt abandoned by God and if Jesus asked "Why?" then it is not so strange if there are times when we have those same feelings and ask those same questions.

The question Jesus asked from the cross comes from Psalm 22, a lament with the elements characteristic of that psalm type. The *complaint* occurs in all three forms. The psalmist complains about enemies:

> All who see me make fun of me;
> they stick out their tongues and shake their heads. . . . (v. 7 TEV)

The psalmist laments his own situation with "I-complaints":

But I am no longer a man; I am a worm. . . .
My strength is gone. . . .
All my bones are out of joint. (vv. 6, 14 TEV)

Most intense is the "you-complaint," addressed
to God:

My God, my God, why have you abandoned me? . . .
During the day I call to you, my God,
but you do not answer. (vv. 1-2 TEV)

Alternating with the complaints are affirmations of *trust* that recall God's goodness in the
past. The psalmist remembers what God has
done for his people:

Our ancestors put their trust in you;
they trusted you, and you saved them. . . .
(v. 4 TEV)

and in his own life,

It was you who brought me safely through
birth. . . .
I have relied on you since the day I was
born,
and you have always been my God.
(vv. 9-10 TEV)

The *requests* are short and to the point:

Do not stay away from me! . . .
Come quickly to my rescue! (vv. 11, 19 TEV)

Then the mood of the psalm changes completely. Because the psalmist is certain the Lord will help, the psalm concludes with a great chorus of *praise,* starting out with, "I will tell my people what you have done. . ." (v. 22 TEV).

How can this psalm, which Jesus prayed on Good Friday, help us with our own Gethsemanes and Good Fridays, with our own times of deepest hurting and most intense questioning?

Psalm 22 encourages us to take our questions, our complaints, and our anger to God. This is all right for Christians to do, because this is what Jesus did when he prayed the psalm. Our prayers do not have to consist only of praise, because our lives do not consist only of happiness.

This psalm invites us to follow along on a path. The starting point is the desperate cry of one who feels abandoned by God, betrayed by friends, and battered by life. Then the psalm suggests that we remember what God has done for us in the past. It invites us to recall our own faithful ancestors; they might have lost a crop, lost a farm, lost a child. But they kept going to church, baptizing their babies, confirming their teenagers, singing the hymns, and praying the prayers. The psalm invites us to remember our own lives and to bring our requests to God: "You've been with me so far, Lord. Now see me through this one, too!"

But what of the final stage along the path of this psalm, the chorus of praise with which it ends? How is it possible to move from the agonized cry with which the psalm begins to the praise with which it ends? For Christians, the answer to that question is given in what happened on Good Friday. Because God gave his Son, there is nothing this world can throw at us that can separate us from God's love in Jesus Christ (Rom. 8:35-39).

Our "Why?" questions may remain questions. So far as we know, even Jesus didn't get an answer to that question asked on the cross. But because of what happened there, the laments emerging from the darkness of a Good Friday afternoon can be transformed into the hallelujahs of a bright Easter morning.

Praise and Lament in the Psalms
The Psalms as Response
In paging through the Psalter, one thing is immediately striking: the great majority of the Psalms are addressed to God. The direction of the Psalms is from people to God. Note the opening words of some psalms:

> I have so many enemies, LORD. . . . (3 TEV)
> Answer me when I pray, O God. . . . (4 TEV)
> Listen to my words, O LORD. . . . (5 TEV)
> LORD, don't be angry and rebuke me! (6 TEV)

This simple observation provides an important clue to understanding the Psalms. The Psalms are the response, the answer of God's people to the words and acts of God.

The writings that make up the Old Testament can be divided into three major categories. First, there are the historical materials, such as the Tetrateuch (Genesis, Exodus, Leviticus, Numbers), the Deuteronomic history (Deuteronomy, Joshua, Judges, 1 and 2 Samuel, 1 and 2 Kings) and the Chronicler's history (1 and 2 Chronicles, Ezra, Nehemiah). Broadly speaking, these books report the mighty acts of God, telling what God has done. Second, there are the prophetic books, which include Isaiah, Jeremiah, and Ezekiel as well as the Book of the Twelve (the Minor Prophets), Hosea through Malachi. The characteristic expression in these books is "Thus says the LORD," followed by a message from the Lord delivered by the prophet. These books report what God has said. The remaining books of the Old Testament are called in the Hebrew Bible the "Writings," and include the Psalms and wisdom literature, such as Job, Proverbs, and Ecclesiastes. These writings present the response of God's people to the words and the acts of God.

The Psalms are the response of God's people. Of all the books of the Bible, they are most directly the people's book. But what shape does that response take? Since the Psalms come from the midst of the lives of real people, we would expect them to reflect the joy and the sorrow that mark the two poles of human existence.

The two major themes running through the Psalms reflect these two poles: Joy brought before God is praise, and sorrow taken to the Lord is lament. Luther recognized these two major themes in the Psalms when he wrote:

> Where does one find finer words of joy than in the psalms of praise and thanksgiving? There you look into the hearts of all the saints, as into fair and pleasant gardens, yes, as into heaven itself. There you see what fine and pleasant flowers of the heart spring up from all sorts of fair and happy thoughts toward God, because of his blessings. On the other hand, where do you find deeper, more sorrowful, more pitiful words of sadness than in the psalms of lamentation? There again you look into the hearts of all the saints, as into death, yes as into hell itself. How gloomy and dark it is there, with all kinds of troubled forebodings about the wrath of God! (*Luther's Works*, vol. 35 [Philadelphia: Fortress, 1960], 255–56)

The Response of Lament

We have already seen that after the introductory psalms, the Psalter presents us with a string of individual laments. There are roughly fifty of these, including Psalms 3; 5; 6; 7; 10; 13; 14; 16; 17; 22; 25; 26; 27:7-14; 28; 31; 35; 36; 38; 39; 40:12-17; 41; 42–43; 51; 52; 53; 54; 55; 56; 57; 58; 59; 61; 63; 64; 69; 71; 77; 86; 88; 94; 102; 109; 120; 130; 140; 141; 142; and 143. There are more individual laments than any other type of psalm in the Psalter. This in itself indicates something: God's people have always been acquainted with trouble and sorrow! These laments indicate how they brought those troubles and sorrows to the Lord. There are also a number of community laments, marked by the pronouns "we" and "us." These include 44; 60; 74; 79; 80; 83; 85; 90; 129; and 137.

The Psalter does not indicate the precise situation out of which each lament comes. A community lament may be occasioned by the destruction of the temple (74). A general description that fits the situation giving rise to the individual laments is found in the title of Psalm 102: "A prayer by a weary sufferer who pours out his complaints to the LORD" (TEV, note). The first chapter of 1 Samuel provides an example of a setting for an individual lament. Hannah is sad because she is childless. She goes to the place of worship and prays, saying to the priest, "I am desperate, and I have been praying, pouring out my troubles to the LORD" (1 Sam. 1:15 TEV). The laments give expression to such a pouring out of troubles and complaints.

When the people of Israel brought their troubles and complaints to the Lord, there was a certain form to their lamenting. We discovered the essential elements of the lament in Psalm 13. The ordering of these elements will vary, and the length of each might be longer or shorter. But they are essential to each lament: *complaint,* in the "I," "they," and "you" form, *request, affirmation of trust,* and *vow to praise.* In such a way, the people of God lamented.

chapter 3

The Way through the Darkness: Psalms of Trust

O LORD, my heart is not lifted up,
  my eyes are not raised too high;
I do not occupy myself with things
  too great and too marvelous for me.
But I have calmed and quieted my soul,
  like a child quieted at its mother's breast;
  like a child that is quieted is my soul.

O Israel, hope in the LORD
  from this time on and for evermore.
                        —Psalm 131 (RSV)

Rock-a-bye Baby (Psalm 131)

I watched with fascination as the drama across from me unfolded. It took place in a small chapel after a day of hiking through the mountains. After singing "Beautiful Savior" and "We Are One in the Spirit," we had just settled back to hear the evening sermon.

Across from me sat a young couple, with a baby sleeping on the wooden bench beside them. First I saw the baby's leg twitch. Next both arms jerked. Then, just as the sermon was getting under way, the child let go with a bloodcurdling cry that caused every head to turn.

I marveled at the efficiency of the parents' response. The father's hand dove for a plastic shoulder bag. Unzipping it, he whipped out a bottle, spun off the retainer ring, stuck the cap in his shirt pocket, flipped the nipple around, and screwed the retainer ring back on, all in the space of that suspense-filled silence when the child, whose face was now a frightening blend of purple and red, was winding up for another wail. He slapped the bottle in the mother's hand, the child's arms flailed at it, pulling the thing into its face, and suddenly all was quiet and heads turned back to catch the next point of the sermon.

When the evening was over, I saw her sitting there, rocking the baby back and forth in her arms, and I heard her singing,

Rock-a-bye baby, in the treetop,
when the wind blows the cradle will rock.

It all reminded me of Psalm 131. This is one of the *psalms of trust;* in order to understand it we should relate it to laments like Psalms 13, 22, and 130. These psalms of trust take the *trust* element in the lament and develop it into an entire psalm.

This one begins with three negative statements:

> O LORD, my heart is not lifted up,
>> my eyes are not raised too high;
> I do not occupy myself with things
>> too great and too marvelous for me. (v. 1)

If my eyes are "raised high," the only way I can see others is to look down my nose at them. This sort of body language is an expression of arrogance or pride, a self-promotion that finally ends up in wanting to take over matters that properly belong to God.

In the next lines, the psalmist owns up to mystery, admitting that there are some questions about life that he cannot answer. The wisdom teachers said the same thing, "Three things are too wonderful for me; four I do not understand" (Prov. 30:18).

Then comes the picture that is the centerpiece of this psalm. A baby who had been kicking and thrashing now lies quietly at its mother's breast. The psalmist sees himself in that picture: he is like the baby, God is like the mother:

> But I have calmed and quieted my soul,
>> like a child quieted at its mother's breast;
>> like a child that is quieted is my soul. (v. 2)

Our nation had its beginning with a Declaration of Independence. Since that time one of the models held before us has been the rugged individualist, the lone cowboy, sitting tall in the saddle, riding confidently into the west, self-sufficient and independent. The model before us in this psalm is quite different. Here we see a child who had been squirming and bleating but who now lies comforted in its mother's arms. This is a picture of our relationship to God. It invites us to something of a Declaration of Dependence.

One of my teachers told this story: A young pilot once succeeded in talking his grandmother into taking her first airplane ride with him in his small private plane. The takeoff went smoothly, and they were soon cruising over the town where she lived. Then her grandson noticed that his passenger was tense and pale and that her knuckles were white as she hung onto the arms of the seat for dear life. When he landed the plane the rest of the family waiting on the ground couldn't wait to get her reaction. "Grandma, how did you like the ride?" they asked. "Oh, it was fine," she said, "but let me tell you a secret. I never really let all my weight down."

The flight would have been so much more enjoyable had she only let her weight down.

This psalm invites us to let our weight down, because "underneath are the everlasting arms" (Deut. 33:27 RSV). It invites us to trust in the Lord, whose arms hold us just as surely as the arms of a lullaby-singing mother hold a beloved child.

The LORD is my shepherd, I shall not want.
   He makes me lie down in green pastures;
he leads me beside still waters;
   he restores my soul.
He leads me in right paths
   for his name's sake.

Even though I walk through the darkest
   valley,
   I fear no evil;
for you are with me;
   your rod and your staff—
   they comfort me.

You prepare a table before me
   in the presence of my enemies;
you anoint my head with oil;
   my cup overflows.
Surely goodness and mercy shall follow me
   all the days of my life.
and I shall dwell in the house of the LORD
   my whole life long.
              —Psalm 23

The Way through the Darkness (Psalm 23)

The quiet student who always sat in the back row of my freshman religion class came up to the desk after my lecture was finished. "Can I ask you a favor?" he began. "My mother is in the hospital.

Do you think you could visit her? She's being operated on tomorrow. My dad isn't living, and she's all alone now."

That evening I stopped by to see her. Her son was sitting on a chair by the bedside. They had obviously been waiting for me. We chatted a bit about her hometown, her work, and her hopes for her son's future. Then she began to talk about the operation. "I've never been in a hospital before," she said, "and I'm afraid." The path of her life was about to lead through the darkness.

I took her hand and began reading the twenty-third psalm. I could feel how she hung on every word. "Even though I walk through the darkest valley, I fear no evil; for you are with me." We prayed and then visited a few more minutes, and I went on my way.

Who could say how many times a scene like this has been repeated? Who could imagine the number of situations where the "Good Shepherd Psalm" has brought a word of comfort to one about to encounter a life-threatening situation? Some of the psalms are suited for the mountain-top experiences of our lives. This one is designed to accompany us when the path that we must take leads through the dark valley.

This psalm of trust is best understood in rela-tionship to the laments. These are the psalms that address the most difficult times in life—when we are asking the hard questions (13), when we are about to go under (130), when we feel forsaken by friends and forgotten by God (22). Psalm 23 comes out of a lament situation. The psalmist is faced with some great danger ("I walk through the valley of the shadow of death") and is surrounded by foes ("in the presence of my enemies"). One of the elements typical of the lament is the affirmation of *trust*. Here that element is developed into an entire psalm.

The movement of the psalm as a whole can be summarized by considering the first, the middle, and the last words: "The LORD . . . with me . . . my whole life long." This notion of the "withness" of God, which is at the center of this psalm, is a powerful theme in the Bible. When the young farmer Gideon was worried about what the future would bring, a messenger from the Lord said, "I will be with you" (Judg. 6:11-16). When Paul's work in Corinth was running into all sorts of opposition, the Lord said, "Do not be afraid . . . for I am with you" (Acts 18:5-11). The name given to the baby Jesus was "Emmanuel," which means "God is with us" (Matt. 1:23). The promise Jesus left with his disciples was, "I am with you always" (Matt. 28:20). The affirmation at the center of this psalm is central to biblical faith: "you are with me."

I remember the time when my young son had his first ten-speed bicycle. It was a Sunday afternoon in the springtime, and we took a ride on the bike path around our town. Just off the path was a drainage tunnel that ran under the interstate highway. We decided to explore it. We parked our bikes and began to walk through the tunnel. It was made of concrete, wide enough for us to walk side by side, but not high enough for me to stand up straight. We walked for a distance, and then the tunnel took a sharp turn and suddenly became dark. A hand reached out and took mine. Neither of us said anything about it, but we continued, hand in hand, until we came to another turn and we could see the light. Then the hand let go.

This is a psalm for those times when the path of our life takes a sharp turn and leads through the darkness. There is no hint that we can avoid the dark valley by taking a detour around it. The path will have to be traveled. But there is a promise that we will never have to go through the darkness alone. Like a good shepherd who cares for the sheep, like a loving parent who holds the hand of a child, the Lord promises to be with us on that way through darkness.

The New Testament makes this promise even stronger. We hear a voice that says, "I am the good shepherd" (John 10:11). And we discover that the hand that holds ours is a hand that has been scarred by the nails of the cross.

* * *

In you, O LORD, I take refuge;
    let me never be put to shame.

In your righteousness deliver me and rescue
    me;
  incline your ear to me and save me.
Be to me a rock of refuge,
  a strong fortress, to save me,
  for you are my rock and my fortress.

Rescue me, O my God, from the hand of
    the wicked,
  from the grasp of the unjust and cruel.
For you, O LORD, are my hope,
  my trust, O LORD, from my youth.
Upon you I have leaned from my birth;
  it was you who took me from my mother's
    womb.
My praise is continually of you.

I have been like a portent to many,
  but you are my strong refuge.
My mouth is filled with your praise,
  and with your glory all day long.
Do not cast me off in the time of old age;
  do not forsake me when my strength is
    spent.
For my enemies speak concerning me,
  and those who watch for my life consult
    together.
They say, "Pursue and seize that person
  whom God has forsaken,
  for there is no one to deliver."

O God, do not be far from me;
　O my God, make haste to help me!
Let my accusers be put to shame and
　　consumed;
　let those who seek to hurt me
　be covered with scorn and disgrace.
But I will hope continually,
　and will praise you yet more and more.
My mouth will tell of your righteous acts,
　of your deeds of salvation all day long,
　　though their number is past my knowledge.
I will come praising the mighty deeds of the
　　Lord God,
　I will praise your righteousness, yours
　　alone.

O God, from my youth you have taught me,
　and I still proclaim your wondrous deeds.
So even to old age and gray hairs,
　O God, do not forsake me,
until I proclaim your might
　to all the generations to come.
Your power and your righteousness, O God,
　reach the high heavens.

You who have done great things,
　O God, who is like you?
You who have made me see many troubles
　　and calamities
　will revive me again;

from the depths of the earth
    you will bring me up again.
You will increase my honor,
    and comfort me once again.
I will also praise you with the harp
    for your faithfulness, O my God;
I will sing praises to you with the lyre,
    O Holy One of Israel.
My lips will shout for joy
    when I sing praises to you;
    my soul also, which you have rescued.
All day long my tongue will talk of your
    righteous help,
for those who tried to do me harm
    have been put to shame, and disgraced.
                —Psalm 71

The Hardest Part Comes Last (Psalm 71)

It was a fall afternoon when my teacher stopped by my office. He had been my professor in college and again in seminary. Now he was visitation pastor at a neighboring church.

I always look forward to a conversation with him. He has a gift for expressing an insight gained from experience in a memorable phrase or two. In biblical times they would have called him a "wise man."

That afternoon he was telling me about calling on the oldest members of his congregation. Our conversation turned to aging. We spoke about retirement centers, geriatric medicine, attitudes toward the elderly. Then he made an observation. "You know," he began, "I've learned that the Lord saves. . . ."

Just at that point my thoughts went racing ahead of his words. I completed his sentence in my mind. "The Lord saves the best part until last," I was sure he would say.

But I was wrong. He surprised me. "You know," he said, "I've learned that the Lord saves the hardest part until last."

The Bible views our life as a journey, a sojourn. The hardest part of the journey is the last part. So said my teacher that day.

It was a spring morning and my students were discussing Psalm 71 in a seminary class. "May I read a poem?" one of them asked. "It has to do with aging," she said, "and with loneliness." The poem was "Minnie Remembers" by Donna Swanson. "Minnie" says, in part:

> How long has it been since someone touched
> me?
> Twenty years? Twenty years I've been a
> widow.
> Respected. Smiled at. But never touched.
> Never held close to another body.
> Never held so close and warm that
> loneliness was blotted out. . . .
> Oh God, I'm so lonely! . . .

God, why didn't we raise the kids
to be silly and affectionate
as well as dignified and proper?
You see, they do their duty.
They drive up in their fine cars.
They come to my room to pay their respects.
They chatter brightly and reminisce.
But they don't touch me. . . .

"The Lord saves the hardest part until last,"
my teacher had said. The poem my student read
said the same thing.

Psalm 71 is the only psalm identified as the
prayer of an old person. "Do not reject me now
that I am old," it asks of the Lord (v. 9 TEV). The
psalmist is going through a difficult time. Those
who should be friends have become enemies:
"They talk and plot against me" (v. 10 TEV). And
what of God? The psalmist is having some
doubts and worries about God. Otherwise why
would he pray, "Do not reject me"?

But, for the most part, this psalm is an affirmation of trust coming from one who has lived a
long life in the faith. "You are my rock and my
fortress," the psalmist says, "my trust, O LORD,
from my youth. Upon you have I leaned from
birth; it was you who took me from my mother's
womb" (vv. 3, 5-6).

It is a winter evening as I write these lines. I
have just returned from visiting a nursing home.

As I stood there waiting for one of the residents, I looked at the gray heads and lined faces in the lounge before me. What stories could each of these people tell? I wondered. What was she like when she was sixteen, laughing, hurrying to meet her boyfriend? What was he like when he was in his thirties, rushing off to watch his son play in a baseball game?

I thought of what my teacher had said about the last part of the journey, and I thought of Minnie's loneliness. Then I recalled some more lines from Psalm 71. This prayer can accompany each of us on our sojourns, from the morning until the evening, from the springtime until the fall of our lives:

O God, from my youth you have taught me,
    and I still proclaim your wondrous deeds.
So even to old age and gray hairs,
    O God, do not forsake me. (vv. 17-18)

* * *

God is indeed good to Israel,
    to those who have pure hearts.
But I had nearly lost confidence;
    my faith was almost gone
because I was jealous of the proud
    when I saw that things go well for the
        wicked.
They do not suffer pain;
    they are strong and healthy.

They do not suffer as other people do;
    they do not have the troubles that others
        have.
And so they wear pride like a necklace
    and violence like a robe;
their hearts pour out evil,
    and their minds are busy with wicked
        schemes.
they laugh at other people and speak of evil
        things;
    they are proud and make plans to oppress
        others.
They speak evil of God in heaven
    and give arrogant orders to men on earth,
so that even God's people turn to them
    and eagerly believe whatever they say.
They say, "God will not know;
    the Most High will not find out."
That is what the wicked are like.
    They have plenty and are always getting
        more.
Is it for nothing, then, that I have kept
        myself pure
    and have not committed sin?
O God, you have made me suffer all day
        long;
    every morning you have punished me.

If I had said such things,
    I would not be acting as one of your people.

I tried to think this problem through,
  but it was too difficult for me
  until I went into your Temple.
Then I understood what will happen to the
    wicked.

You will put them in slippery places
  and make them fall to destruction!
They are instantly destroyed;
  they go down to a horrible end.
They are like a dream that goes away in the
    morning;
  when you rouse yourself, O LORD, they
    disappear.

When my thoughts were bitter
  and my feelings were hurt,
I was as stupid as an animal;
  I did not understand you.
Yet I always stay close to you,
  and you hold me by the hand.
You guide me with your instruction
  and at the end you will receive me with
    honor.
What else do I have in heaven but you?
  Since I have you, what else could I want
    on earth?
My mind and my body may grow weak,
  but God is my strength;
  he is all I ever need.

Those who abandon you will certainly perish;
   you will destroy those who are unfaithful
      to you.
But as for me, how wonderful to be near
   God,
   to find protection with the LORD God
   and to proclaim all that he has done!
                              —Psalm 73 (TEV)

When Good Things Happen to Bad People (Psalm 73)

"It isn't fair," she said.

She was talking to me about her son. We had just left him at the hospital, and she was giving me a ride home.

"I wish it had happened to me," she went on. "He has his whole life ahead of him. He's such a good person."

She was right. He was a good person. I had known him since he was a boy. One of the faithfuls in Sunday school and the youth group, he had spent the past summer working as a camp counselor. His trumpet playing had enriched many a Christmas and Easter service. Now he was a college senior, preparing to become a teacher. But he had suddenly taken ill, and they had to fly him home. The outlook was uncertain.

I saw her reach for a handkerchief and wipe a tear from her eye. I had known her for years but had never seen her cry before. Nor was she one to complain. But she said it again, "I don't understand it. It just isn't fair!"

That mother was not the first person to question the fairness of our world. A whole chorus of others, including the sturdiest of believers, have asked, "Why do bad things happen to good people?"

Among those questioners is the writer of Psalm 73. The thing that was bothering him was his illness. He lived with a pain that a good night's sleep could not take away:

> For all day long I have been plagued,
>   and am punished every morning.

He came very close to losing his faith:

> But as for me, my feet had almost stumbled;
>   my steps had nearly slipped.

He wondered whether the religion he had lived all his life had been a waste of time:

> All in vain I have kept my heart clean
>   and washed my hands in innocence.

What drove this person to such a low point? What caused these doubts and this despair? What made him say, "It isn't fair"? He knew he was a decent and good person, yet he was hurting badly. He could think of many liars and cheaters, scoundrels and adulterers who were healthy as horses and sound as shekels. He tells about them:

> They do not suffer pain;
>> they are strong and healthy. . . .
>> they do not have the troubles that others
>>> have.
> They say, "God will not know;
>> the Most High will not find out."
> . . . They have plenty and are always getting
>> more. (vv. 4-5, 11-12 TEV)

The psalmist tried to figure it all out: Bad things happen to good people, and good things happen to bad people. The more he thought about it, the worse he felt (v. 16). At least he didn't share his doubts with others, because he thought that might be bad for the children (v. 15)! It was enough to make a person give up on God—almost.

Then one day it all changed. His ordinary routine took him to a worship service. He sat down with some of his old friends. They sang the old hymns and prayed the familiar prayers. They heard a familiar story from the Bible. Afterward several asked, "How are you getting along?" And his perspective changed. He tells us that he had been sliding downward into an abyss of doubt and despair, "until I went into the sanctuary of God" (v. 17 RSV).

True, bad things happen to good people; this good person had experienced them. And good things happen to bad people; he could furnish some examples. But as the community gathered together in worship, he heard some things that he had forgotten. Despite the unfairness of the world, he said to God:

Nevertheless I am continually with you;
   you hold my right hand.
My flesh and my heart may fail,
   but God is the strength of my heart
   and my portion forever. (vv. 23, 26)

The psalmist fired this great "nevertheless" in the face of all that the world could throw at him. With this he joined that apostle who knew something of hurting and pain, but who also knew that no matter what happened, nothing could separate us from the love of God in Christ Jesus our Lord (Rom. 8:35-39).

* * *

God is our refuge and strength,
   a very present help in trouble.
Therefore we will not fear, though the earth
      should change,
   though the mountains shake in the heart
      of the sea;
though its waters roar and foam,
   though the mountains tremble with its
      tumult.

There is a river whose streams make glad
      the city of God,

the holy habitation of the Most High.
God is in the midst of the city, it shall not
    be moved;
  God will help it when the morning dawns.
The nations are in an uproar, the kingdoms
    totter,
  he utters his voice, the earth melts.
The LORD of hosts is with us;
  the God of Jacob is our refuge.

Come, behold the works of the LORD;
  see what desolations he has brought on
    the earth.
He makes wars cease to the end of the earth;
  he breaks the bow, and shatters the spear;
  he burns the shields with fire.
"Be still, and know that I am God!
  I am exalted among the nations,
  I am exalted in the earth."
The LORD of hosts is with us;
  the God of Jacob is our refuge.
               —Psalm 46

The Trumpet Every Morning (Psalm 46)

He came down the stairs into the living room
where we were gathered, carrying a battered,
once-golden trumpet in his hand. He had been a
pastor in a small town in what was then East Germany for more than forty years. Now he was
retired. He and his wife, like my wife and me,

were guests at a friend's home in another German town.

After we were introduced, he started telling us about the trumpet. He had played it in brass choirs in Germany for more than fifty years now, he said. Then he told of his daily routine.

"Our parsonage is right across the street from the courthouse," he began, "where all the communist leaders of our town have their offices. Each morning at exactly eight o'clock I open the window toward the courthouse, take out my trumpet, and play the two hymns our hymnbook assigns for the day. I've been doing this for years. It's a reminder of our faith for the people working there and for anyone else who happens to be listening."

"Would you play for us?" I asked. "Of course," he said, and took the trumpet out into the garden. The first hymn I didn't recognize. The second I did; it was "A Mighty Fortress Is Our God."

As he played, I wondered: How many times has he sent that battle hymn of the Reformation out into the open air of East Germany? What memories does that melody evoke in the hearts of those who hear it? Memories of confirmation, of choirs, or church services? What thoughts go through the head of even the most ardent Marxist when he or she hears that trumpet every morning?

"A mighty fortress is our God, a sword and shield victorious." That was one of the hymns that carried the Reformation along on its melody and words. It was Luther's paraphrase of Psalm 46.

The dominant note in the forty-sixth psalm is trust. Psalm 23, the most well-known of the psalms of trust, uses the picture of the Lord as a shepherd. That psalm is between the individual and God: "The LORD is *my* shepherd, *I* shall not want. . . . *I* fear no evil; for you are with *me*." This psalm of trust is different. This one is between God and the people. The pronouns are all plural. This is a psalm to be said, prayed, and sung shoulder to shoulder, standing alongside other believers:

> God is *our* refuge and strength,
>   a very present help in trouble.
> Therefore *we* will not fear,
>   though the earth should change,
>   though the mountains shake in the heart
>   of the sea. (vv. 1-2)

This time God is not pictured as a shepherd, but as a fortress, a refuge, a high place in the cliffs, where neither nature nor human foe can cause any harm. The refrain continues the note of trust:

> The LORD of hosts is with *us;*
>   the God of Jacob is *our* refuge. (vv. 7, 11)

The Lutheran church has assigned this psalm to the service for the burial of the dead. It is to be called upon in the most difficult of times. When the relatives of the deceased are gathered under a canopy at some cemetery, when the rain is driving down and the wind is whipping the canvas so that the preacher can hardly be heard, when all are wondering what life will be like without that person—this is the time for Psalm 46. This is the time for the little company gathered there to confess together, "God is our refuge and strength, a very present help in trouble."

This is one of the psalms that believers have always turned to when the going is the toughest. Luther knew that, when he wrote in the final stanza of his famous hymn, "A Mighty Fortress Is Our God":

> Were they to take our house,
> Goods, honor, child, or spouse,
> Though life be wrenched away,
> They cannot win the day.
> The Kingdom's ours forever!

The psalm's refrain declares, "The LORD of hosts is with us. . . ." That line was transposed into a new key with the birth of Jesus, named Emmanuel, or "God is with us" (Matt. 1:23). The good news about Jesus is worth preaching about, singing about, even blowing a trumpet about.

They blew the trumpets at Jericho for only seven days and the walls came tumbling down. We know, of course, that the wall separating

East and West Germany finally did come down, in November 1989. Who knows what changes occurred in that small town in East Germany because of the trumpet that was sounded at precisely eight o'clock each morning?

The psalms of trust, we have seen, are closely related to the laments. They take one element of the lament, the affirmation of trust, and develop it into an entire psalm. Whether a psalm should be classified as a lament or a psalm of trust is at times a matter of judgment. Those that are usually considered individual psalms of trust include 4; 23; 27:1-6; 62; 73; and 131. Psalms 46; 123; 125; and 126 may be considered community psalms of trust.

chapter 4

Psalms for Sojourners: The Pilgrimage Psalms

I lift up my eyes to the hills—
  from where will my help come?
My help comes from the LORD,
  who made heaven and earth.

He will not let your foot be moved;
  he who keeps you will not slumber.
He who keeps Israel
  will neither slumber nor sleep.

The LORD is your keeper;
  the LORD is your shade at your right hand.
The sun shall not strike you by day,
  nor the moon by night.

The LORD will keep you from all evil;
  he will keep your life.
The LORD will keep
  your going out and your coming in
  from this time on and forevermore.
                —Psalm 121

A Psalm for Sojourners (Psalm 121)

We all know that fleeting moment of anxiety that comes just at the outset of a long journey. The car is packed, the family is in place, the seat belts are fastened. But just before you turn the key in the ignition, there is that question lurking in the back of your mind: Will we arrive safely, without an accident? Or perhaps: the plane has taxied to the end of the runway, the flight attendants are seated in their places, and the 747 begins to roll toward takeoff. You look out the window and wonder for a moment: Will this be another safe flight?

Psalm 121 begins with such an anxious traveler's question. It is one of a group of *pilgrimage psalms* (120–134), which originated to accompany those making the journey to Jerusalem for one of the great festivals (Deut. 16:16).

This psalm originated as a short liturgy for times of saying good-bye. The person about to leave looks toward the mountains in the distance and asks: "I lift up my eyes to the hills—from where will my help come?" Then the traveler himself answers the question with a confession of faith: "My help comes from the LORD, who made heaven and earth." The traveler's God is not too small! That God, after all, made those mountains and the white clouds and blue sky above them.

In the second part, those staying behind address the traveler with words of encouragement:

He will not let your foot be moved;
    he who keeps you will not slumber.
he who keeps Israel
    will neither slumber nor sleep. (vv. 3-4)

The traveler had confessed faith in God, the Creator of heaven and earth. Now the focus begins to narrow: the traveler's friends declare that this Creator is concerned about Israel, and that he even cares about *you*.

The word *keep* is part of the biblical vocabulary describing the activity of a watchman. The main requirement for a watchman is staying awake! Isaiah 56:10 tells of some worthless watchmen who love to sleep. But the Lord is the Good Watchman (the picture also occurs in Ps. 127:1) who does not doze off. Luther comments on this psalm, saying that it teaches "that we should remain steadfast and await God's help and protection. Because even though it appears that God is sleeping or snoring . . . this is certainly not so. . . . He is surely awake and watching over us" (*D. Martin Luthers Psalmen Auslegung,* vol. 3, ed. Erwin Mülhaupt [Göttingen: Vandenhoeck and Ruprecht, 1965], 599; my translation).

The speaker in the psalm continues: The Lord, the Good Watchman, will protect the traveler from the dangers of the day—the hot sun—and the perils of the night—the moon, thought to have ill effects on people. Mendelssohn caught the sense of this psalm in the chorus from his oratorio *Elijah:* "He, watching over Israel, slumbers not nor sleeps."

In the last part of the psalm an amazing thing happens. The watching and "keeping" of the Lord is expanded to include not only the journey but a lifetime:

> The LORD will keep you from all evil;
>   he will keep your life.
> The LORD will keep
>   your going out and your coming in
>   from this time on and forevermore.
>   (vv. 7-8)

The expression "going out and . . . coming in" refers to all the activities of one's daily living (Deut. 28:6). Thus, this farewell liturgy concludes with the assurance that the Lord will watch over the traveler not only for this journey but for the whole journey of life.

Life as a journey, a sojourn—we might prefer some other image. A scene: It was springtime, the first day of sunshine after a long and dreary winter. A son was home from England; a daughter had stopped by. The three of us took a football and a new puppy to the park across the way and loosened up muscles that had been dormant over the winter. I stopped for a moment to catch my breath and watched them, two grown children and a puppy, running and laughing in the sunshine. It would be nice to hold onto this time, I thought, but I knew that in an hour he would head back to college and she to her own home.

Life is not like a circle, with possessions at the outer boundaries, then friends, then family, and in the center "just Molly and me and baby makes three," as the old song had it. No, the Bible views our life as a journey, and the melody running through it is a more bracing tune, closer to the spirit of Willie Nelson's "On the Road Again." The call of Jesus was not "Gather around me," but rather, "Follow me."

The church has long recognized that this psalm embraces the entire journey of life. In an old Norwegian baptismal liturgy, the pastor blessed the person being baptized with a paraphrase of verse 8: "The Lord preserve thy coming in and thy going out from this time forth and forevermore." In the newest Lutheran services, the psalm finds a place at the other extreme of life, as part of the service of burial.

Psalm 121 remains a psalm appropriate for the traveler, whether that traveler reaches down to fasten a sandal strap or reaches over to fasten a seat belt. But it also is a psalm suited for the whole of life's way, for all our comings and goings, from baptism to burial. Such is the psalm for sojourners.

* * *

Unless the LORD builds the house,
  those who build it labor in vain.
Unless the LORD guards the city,
  the guard keeps watch in vain.
It is in vain that you rise up early
  and go late to rest,
eating the bread of anxious toil;
  for he gives sleep to his beloved.

Sons are indeed a heritage from the LORD,
  the fruit of the womb a reward.
Like arrows in the hand of a warrior
  are the sons of one's youth.
Happy is the man who has
  his quiver full of them.
He shall not be put to shame
  when he speaks with his enemies in the
    gate.

—Psalm 127

A Word for Worriers and Workaholics (Psalm 127)

Perhaps you know the type. He is the first to get to the office in the morning and the last to leave at night. "It sets a good example for the others," he tells himself. He never uses all his vacation days. His lunch usually is an egg-salad sandwich eaten at his desk. On Saturdays he's more relaxed, wearing cords and an old sweater, but he's still at the office. His style of life has added a new word to our language. He is a "workaholic," one who is addicted to work, who eats, drinks, and sleeps his job.

You may recognize the type. She just can't seem to relax and enjoy herself. The last thoughts she shares with her husband at the end of the day run down the agenda of her concerns: Should we talk to Jennifer's teacher about her problem in math? Do you think you can remember to check that noise in the car tomorrow? What will the neighbors think if we are not there? She has trouble getting to sleep, and she is waking up earlier and earlier, believing that it is her duty to baby-sit the entire world. Her problem is worry.

These are not new concerns. Psalm 127 addresses both of them. Another of the pilgrimage psalms gathered in Psalms 120–134, its everyday themes and uncomplicated piety testify to its origin in the lives of God's people who lived in the country, some distance from the capital city of Jerusalem.

The psalm begins with three short sayings, each describing an activity judged to be "in vain" (NRSV) or "useless" (TEV). "Unless the LORD builds the house, those who build it labor in *vain*." The dreaming, planning, building that go into the creation of a new home should all be done under the Lord's guidance and blessing. That is the viewpoint of this psalm. We still detect something of this attitude in our prayers for the blessing of a new home (such as those in *Occasional Services: A Companion to Lutheran Book of Worship* [Minneapolis: Augsburg, 1982], 186–91).

"Unless the Lord watches over the city, the watchman stays awake *in vain.*" High up on the outer wall of the courthouse in Leipzig, Germany, in full view of those in the center of the city, are the words of the first verse of this psalm. Whoever designed and built that courthouse knew that the best provisions for community safety and security are of no use unless the city's leaders are men and women who know they are discharging their duties as those appointed by God (Rom. 13:1).

"It is in vain that you rise up early and go late to rest, eating the bread of anxious toil; for he gives sleep to his beloved" (v. 2). This is not a negative word concerning work. In contrast to other creation stories from the ancient world, the Bible, starting with the creation story, views work in a positive way. Even in paradise, before sin came into the picture, the first human being was charged with tilling and keeping the garden (Gen. 2:15). The book of Proverbs warns young people against laziness and admonishes them to work hard: "Go to the ant, you lazybones; consider its ways, and be wise" (Prov. 6:6). "A slack hand causes poverty, but the hand of the diligent makes rich" (Prov. 10:4). Paul paid his own way as a tentmaker (Acts 18:3). Jesus was known as "the carpenter" (Mark 6:3).

I once heard a story about Golda Meir, late prime minister of Israel, and her visit with the pope. She found it quite remarkable, she told him, that the daughter of a poor carpenter from Milwaukee should have a chance to meet with the Holy Father. The pope said, "Mrs. Meir, let me assure you that we hold the profession of carpentry in high regard around here." That statement well expresses the biblical-Christian attitude toward all constructive work.

This third "in vain" saying does not say that work is useless. It does say that the frantic, seven-days-a-week addiction to work that we call "workaholism" is a style of life not appropriate for God's children. The Lord himself created the whole universe in six days and found time to rest on the seventh. The point of Gen. 2:1-4 is that the Lord's taking time for Sabbath rest is an example for our own division of labor and rest.

Psalm 127 also addresses anxiety or worry. Jesus spoke to that subject: "Do not be worried about the food and drink you need in order to stay alive, or about clothes for your body. . . . Look at the birds flying around: they do not plant seeds, gather a harvest and put it in barns; yet your Father in heaven takes care of them! Aren't you worth much more than birds? Can any of you live a bit longer by worrying about it?" (Matt. 6:25-26

TEV). The old gospel song has it right: "I sing because I'm happy, I sing because I'm free. His eye is on the sparrow, and I know he watches me."

"For he gives to his beloved sleep," the saying concludes. In Charles Peguy's poem "Sleep," God says, "Sleep is perhaps the most beautiful thing I have created. And I myself rested on the seventh day." The poem continues, with God still speaking:

> Poor people, they don't know what is good.
> They look after their business very well
>   during the day.
> But they haven't enough confidence in me
>   to let me look after it during the night.
> As if I wasn't capable of looking
>   after it during one night. . . .
> And I say Blessed, blessed is the man
>   who puts off what he has to
>   do until tomorrow.
> Blessed is he who puts off.
>   That is to say, Blessed is he who hopes.
>   And who sleeps.

Home, community, work, and sleep. Such are the ordinary but essential themes of this psalm for sojourners.

* * *

> How wonderful it is, how pleasant,
>   for God's people to live together in
>   harmony!

It is like the precious anointing oil
   running down from Aaron's head and
      beard,
   down to the collar of his robes.
It is like the dew on Mount Hermon,
   falling on the hills of Zion.
That is where the Lord has promised his
      blessing—
   life that never ends.

                              —Psalm 133 (TEV)

Where It All Comes Together (Psalm 133)

On a Saturday morning in September I aimed my Chevrolet toward the white frame church that stood on a hill rising above the surrounding prairie. The sky was blue and the air was clear with the crisp smell of fall in it. I turned in and noticed the dew glistening on the grass of the churchyard.

"Good morning, pastor," someone said, and I walked toward the church and joined a group of men standing there. They were talking about the fishing "up north." "One hundred and twenty walleyes in three days," one of them said. "Next year in Jerusalem," thinks the Jew. "Next year in Canada," dreams the fisherman, and I jotted down the name of a resort and resolved to take my boys there—next year.

A smiling woman pinned a flower on me and ushered me through a door and into the sanctuary.

It was the congregation's annual spiritual emphasis weekend, and the people kept coming, waving, greeting one another: men and women, teenagers, little children.

"We always start with some singing," an usher told me, and the song leader appeared. A construction worker by trade, he was one of those people destined to be song leaders, with music in his bones and the kind of enthusiasm found only in those who are not professional musicians. He called out the directions: "Now just the men. . . . Now the women. . . ." His daughter was at the piano, and the two of them worked together with perfect timing, evidence they had done all this before.

As the singing went on, I knew something authentic was happening here. Here it all came together. Here these people gathered for baptisms and burials, for confirmations and weddings, and now for study and praise.

Psalm 133 describes such a gathering of God's people. It is another one of the pilgrimage psalms (120–134), originally intended for use in connection with journeys to Jerusalem for the annual festivals. It begins with a short saying that describes the happiness of a family gathering.

How wonderful it is, how pleasant,
when brothers and sisters live together in
    harmony! (my translation)

How did this saying grow into a psalm? Maybe it happened on a crisp, fall day in Jerusalem. Perhaps some of the men were standing outside the temple telling stories about the fishing "up north." Inside they were starting to sing the old familiar psalms. Then along came someone with an eye for beauty and an ear for music and took it all in: the glistening of the dew, the gathering of families and friends, the sound of the singing, the scent of the oil used for installing a priest. The saying about the family was transformed into a saying about the family of God, and a psalm was born:

How wonderful it is, how pleasant,
> for God's people to live together in
> harmony!
It is like the precious anointing oil
> running down from Aaron's head and
> beard,
> down to the collar of his robes.
It is like the dew of Mount Hermon,
> falling on the hills of Zion. (TEV)

Here, as they gathered for worship, it all came together.

What of our own lives? Where does it all come together for us? Most of the time, it may seem, our lives are not coming together but flying apart. The harried young mothers and fathers spend their days taxiing carloads of children to

Girl Scouts, Boy Scouts, piano lessons, swimming lessons, meetings at school, meetings at church. The gatherings of our families and extended families become fewer and fewer as the children leave home and the years go by. It seems we are always sending someone off somewhere and saying good-bye.

Nor do our jobs bring us together. The paths of our working lives are like spokes on a wheel, moving out from the center, becoming increasingly distant from one another. We become more and more expert at the intricacies of the computer or the subtleties of corporation law, and discover that we have less and less to talk about with the people next door. The pressures and stresses of modern living do not pull us together but drive us apart.

Is there a center, a place of calm, a time that could be compared to the scent of expensive perfume or the sight of the morning dew? This psalm suggests that there is. That center is the gathering of the family of God for worship. The New Testament does not quote Psalm 133, but family language is on almost every one of its pages. Jesus said, "For whoever does the will of my Father in heaven is my brother and sister and mother" (Matt. 12:50). Paul uses family language when he writes about his friends, referring to them as "sister Phoebe" or "brother Quartus" (Romans 16; see vv. 1, 23).

Some Sunday morning you may be a bit late getting to church. Your first instinct will be to park the car, slam the door, and race toward the building. But instead, pause for a moment. Maybe you will catch the sound of a familiar hymn. Perhaps you will notice the dew glistening in the morning sun. Someone may greet you with a "good morning" and a smile. Then, as you slip into the back pew and join in the last verse of "Praise to the Lord, the Almighty," you may discover what the psalmist was talking about: "How wonderful it is, how pleasant, for God's people to live together in harmony."

The Pilgrimage Psalms
The Heading
Psalms 120–134 each have the heading, "A Song of Ascents." This heading is an apparent reference to ascending or "going up" to Jerusalem for the annual festivals held there: "Three times a year all your males shall appear before the Lᴏʀᴅ your God at the place that he will choose: at the festival of unleavened bread, at the festival of weeks, and at the festival of booths" (Deut. 16:16). Since Jerusalem is situated high in the mountains, the biblical expression for going there is to "go up" (1 Kings 12:28; Ps. 122:4; Isa. 2:3; Luke 2:42; and so forth). These psalms once existed as a separate collection, a kind of hymnbook and prayer book for the use of those

making a pilgrimage to the Holy City. Thus they may be called *pilgrimage psalms*.

The Origins

Psalm 120 assumes the situation of one who is far away from Jerusalem, living in the wilderness of Arabia (v. 5). Psalm 121, as we have seen, is a liturgy for saying good-bye to the pilgrims as they set out. Psalm 122 reflects the excitement and joy of those about to make the trip: "I was glad when they said to me, 'Let us go to the house of the LORD!'" (v. 1). Psalm 133 expresses the happiness of being together with other worshipers: "How wonderful it is, how pleasant, for God's people to live together in harmony!" (v. 1, TEV).

The psalms in this group give evidence of origins in the villages and the countryside. We have noted that the writer of Psalm 120 is in Arabia; Psalm 126 mentions the Negeb in the south, and Psalm 133 refers to Hermon in the north. The imagery in them is drawn from farming (126:5-6; 129:3, 6-7), hunting and warfare (120:4-7; 124:6-7), labor (127:1), and especially from the family (123:2; 127:3-5; 128:3-6; 131:2). One author has concluded that the world of these psalms

> is the world of the simple person and the little people, of the farmer, the handworker,

the mother with small children, the father of the family who works from early until late, who experiences both tears and jubilation, who rejoices at the festivals and thinks about religious matters. These psalms are witnesses from everyday life, witnesses of folk poetry and folk piety. All of this makes them especially precious. (Klaus Seybold, *Die Wallfahrtspsalmen* [Neukirchen-Vluyn: Neukirchener Verlag, 1978], 42; my translation)

The Piety

What are the marks of the "folk piety" that these psalms express? The God to whom they witness is the mighty Creator of the heavens and the earth (121:2; 124:8; 134:3). This God is also the Deliverer who has rescued Israel in warfare (124; 126:1-3) and to whom the people pray to rescue them again (125:4-5; 126:4-6; 129:5-8). But this is also the God who is close at hand, who cares about the everyday concerns of his people, who blesses them with those things needed for a happy and successful life. The Lord prospers them in their work (127:1; 128:2) and watches over them in their sleep (121:6; 127:2). He provides them with food (128:2) and protects them on their travels (121). God gives his people the happiness of family life (127:3-5) and the joy of watching their young ones grow up around their table (128:3-4). The people of these psalms know the laughter of celebration (126:1-3, 6) and the gladness of gathering for worship (122:1; 133). They also know the depths of despair, but even in these depths, they still hope in the Lord (130). They put their trust in the Lord, mighty as the mountains around Jerusalem (125), caring as a good master or mistress (123). They know that their lives can be lived out in calm and peace, like the life of a child resting quietly in its mother's arms (131).

Luther summarized these psalms by saying that they "deal with important teaching and almost all of the articles of our Christian faith, of preaching, forgiveness of sins, the cross, love, marriage, authorities, so that they set forth as it were a summary of all essential teachings" (*D. Martin Luthers Psalmen Auslegung,* vol. 3, ed. Erwin Mülhaupt [Göttingen: Vandenhoeck and Ruprecht, 1965], 599; my translation).

Such are these psalms of the ordinary people, these psalms for pilgrims and for sojourners.

chapter 5

From King David to Duke Ellington: The Hymns

Praise the Lord!
Praise, O servants of the Lord;
   praise the name of the Lord.

Blessed be the name of the Lord
   from this time on and forevermore.
From the rising of the sun to its setting
   the name of the Lord is to be praised.
The Lord is high above all nations,
   and his glory above the heavens.

Who is like the Lord our God,
   who is seated on high,
who looks far down
   on the heavens and the earth?
he raises the poor from the dust,
   and lifts the needy from the ash heap,
to make them sit with princes,
   with the princes of his people.

He gives the barren woman a home,
　　making her the joyous mother of children.
Praise the LORD!

　　　　　　　　　　　　　—Psalm 113

Sunrise, Sunset (Psalm 113)

Like all parents at weddings, these two are nostalgic. They look at the bride and groom and marvel at how quickly the years have gone by. The scene is the marriage of the daughter of Tevye and Golde in *Fiddler on the Roof.* Tevye asks, "Is this the little girl I carried? Is this the little boy at play?"

Golde responds, "I don't remember growing older. When did they?" Then the guests join in singing,

> Sunrise, sunset,
> Sunrise, sunset,
> Swiftly fly the years.
> One season following another,
> Laden with happiness and tears.

Happiness and tears. These represent the two poles of our lives, the good times and the bad, the joys and the sorrows. The Psalms reflect these two poles. Sorrow is taken to the Lord in the laments. Joy is brought before God in the *hymns,* or psalms of praise.

Psalm 113 is a good example of a hymn. It begins with a *call to praise:*

Praise the Lord!
Praise, O servants of the Lord,
   praise the name of the Lord!

The psalmist thinks big. He calls for the Lord's praise to resound through all time, from now to eternity:

Blessed be the name of the Lord
   from this time on and forevermore. (v. 2)

The call also goes out for praise to roll across all space. The psalm speaks of the sunrise and the sunset, meaning the east and the west:

From the rising of the sun to its setting
   the name of the Lord is to be praised.
   (v. 3)

But *why* praise the Lord? The next part of the psalm provides some *reasons for praise.* First, because the Lord is great and there is no other God:

The Lord is high above all nations,
   and his glory above the heavens.
Who is like the Lord our God,
   who is seated on high. (vv. 4-5)

The psalm continues with another reason for praise. God is great, but God is also good. The psalm illustrates God's goodness with two pictures, each providing a reason for praising God. Imagine a man who has been fired, who has lost self-esteem, and who considers himself a failure. Then comes an unexpected telephone call and he is offered a job. He is happy in his new work. One day he looks back at these events in his life and can only thank and praise God for what has happened:

> [God] raises the poor from the dust,
> and lifts the needy from the ash heap.
> (v. 7)

Consider a young wife who has wanted more than anything to have a baby. For years she and her husband have continued childless. Then she discovers she is pregnant, and a baby is born! In a few years another child arrives. One evening she looks at her children happily playing together, and she can only thank and praise God for them:

> [God] gives the barren woman a home,
> making her the joyous mother of children.
> (v. 9)

The psalm begins and ends with "Praise the LORD!"—which in Hebrew is "Hallelujah!" The chorus of hallelujahs, which God's people have been singing since Old Testament times, was transposed into a new key with the events of Good Friday and Easter. Since then, there has been a new reason for praising God. God is great and God is good, and his goodness takes its most dramatic expression in the sending of his Son to deliver us from our sins.

We hear those hallelujahs each Easter Sunday: "Christ the Lord is risen today; Hallelujah!" And I can still hear a college choir singing about some farmers in Russia, doing their field work to the accompaniment of a song:

> Peasants on their farms are singing
>> As the oxen munch their feed.
> Alleluia! Christ is risen,
>> Christ the Lord is risen indeed!

* * *

> Bless the LORD, O my soul,
>> and all that is within me,
>> bless his holy name.
> Bless the LORD, O my soul,
>> and do not forget all his benefits—
> who forgives all your iniquity,
>> who heals all your diseases,
> who redeems your life from the Pit,
>> who crowns you with steadfast love and mercy,
> who satisfies you with good as long as you live
>> so that your youth is renewed like the eagle's.

> The LORD works vindication
>> and justice for all who are oppressed.

He made known his ways to Moses,
   his acts to the people of Israel.
The LORD is merciful and gracious,
   slow to anger and abounding in steadfast
      love.
He will not always accuse,
   nor will he keep his anger forever.
He does not deal with us according to our
   sins,
   nor repay us according to our iniquities.
For as the heavens are high above the earth,
   so great is his steadfast love toward those
      who fear him;
as far as the east is from the west,
   so far he removed our transgressions from
      us.
As a father has compassion for his children,
   so the LORD has compassion for those who
      fear him.
For he knows how we were made;
   he remembers that we are dust.

As for mortals, their days are like grass;
   they flourish like a flower of the field;
for the wind passes over it, and it is gone,
   and its place knows it no more.
But the steadfast love of the Lord is from
     everlasting to everlasting
   on those who fear him,
   and his righteousness to children's children,

to those who keep his covenant
and remember to do his commandments.

The LORD has established his throne in the
heavens,
and his kingdom rules over all.
Bless the LORD, O you his angels,
you mighty ones who do his bidding,
obedient to his spoken word.
Bless the LORD, all his hosts,
his ministers that do his will.
Bless the LORD, all his works,
in all places of his dominion.
Bless the LORD, O my soul.
—Psalm 103

Time to Remember (Psalm 103)
This psalm is an invitation to take time to
remember. "Bless the LORD . . . and do not forget
all his benefits," it begins. And remembering, it
suggests, leads to praise and to thanksgiving.

Remember that God forgives your sins. The
psalm suggests that we recall those times of
which we are not proud: that unkind treatment
of a neighbor, that unnecessary act of cruelty
toward a friend, that carrying of a grudge for
months and for years, that unfaithfulness to a
husband or a wife. Then the psalm recalls some
astonishing news: "Despite what you've done,
because of Jesus Christ, you are forgiven. You are

accepted. Now accept the fact that you are accepted." Don't forget the benefits of the Lord, "who forgives all your iniquity" (v. 3).

Remember that God heals your sicknesses and rescues you from death. Recall a time when you and your spouse sat late into the night watching and praying as a newborn baby struggled for breath and life. Then the fever broke, the heartbeat slowed, and the breathing became regular. You thanked God, "who heals all your diseases, who redeems your life from the Pit" (v. 3).

And don't forget the good things you enjoy each day: a loving family, a faithful friend, food and clothing, a home, a job, freedom. Such are the gifts of a God who "satisfies you with good as long as you live" (v. 5).

The Lord "forgives your iniquity" and "heals all your diseases." In other words, the Lord deals with our failures and with our frailty. The remainder of the psalm spells out these themes.

What of our *failures?* Verse 8 expresses the foundation upon which the whole psalm is built: "The Lord is merciful and gracious, slow to anger and abounding in steadfast love." The word *merciful* is related to the Hebrew for *womb.* The picture is of God's love that surrounds and supports, just as a child is surrounded and supported in a mother's womb. God's love is also like the love of a father: "As kind as a father is to his children, so kind is the LORD" (v. 13 TEV). The story that

Jesus told about the father who never stopped loving a rebelling son is a sermon on this text (Luke 15:11-32).

I recall hearing a recording of a sermon given by the American preacher and theologian Reinhold Niebuhr. He was speaking of the grace of God. He told of a professor and his wife who had taken a young foster child into their family. They knew that the boy was reputed to be a terror, and they were prepared for the worst. Billy wouldn't go to bed at night and he wouldn't get up in the morning. He used foul language. At breakfast one morning he threw a dish of oatmeal at one of the other children. But the family kept their cool and took it all in stride.

Then one afternoon the professor came home from teaching and was alarmed to see the garden hose stuck through the living room window. The water was turned on full blast. He ran to shut it off. Then he saw the boy watching him. He walked over, put his hand on the lad's shoulder and said, "Billy, how long is it going to take you to learn that we are going to keep on loving you, no matter what you do?" That kind of love, said the preacher, is called grace. Such is the love of which this psalm speaks.

Finally, the psalm addresses our *frailty*. The Creator is aware of our limitations: "For he knows how we were made; he remembers that we are dust" (v. 14). The psalmist knew that while

God heals our diseases, he does not heal every disease. We are not immortal. He knew that God rescues us from death, but that finally we will fade and die: "As for us, our life is like grass. We grow and flourish like a wild flower; then the wind blows on it, and it is gone" (v. 15 TEV). Nevertheless, he speaks of God's love that holds us close "from everlasting to everlasting" (v. 17). The apostle would add that nothing, not even death, can separate us from that love (Rom. 8:38). The hymn writer put it this way:

> We blossom and flourish like leaves on the tree,
> And wither and perish, but naught changeth thee.
>
> (*Lutheran Book of Worship* 526, stanza 3)

"We are dust," says the psalm. We are not angels, nor are we gods. But we are God's, and his love forgives our failures and outlasts our frailties. Since the resurrection of Jesus, we have an idea of what we can hope for (1 Corinthians 15).

This psalm encourages us to pause and take time to remember all the Lord's benefits and then to praise and give thanks: "Bless the LORD, O my soul" (v. 22).

* * *

Praise the LORD!
Praise God in his sanctuary;
   praise him in his mighty firmament!

Praise him for his mighty deeds;
   praise him according to his surpassing
      greatness!

Praise him with trumpet sound;
   praise him with lute and harp!
Praise him with tambourine and dance;
   praise him with strings and pipe!
Praise him with clanging cymbals;
   praise him with loud clashing cymbals!
Let everything that breathes praise the LORD!
Praise the LORD!

—Psalm 150

From King David to Duke Ellington (Psalm 150)

It was one o'clock in the morning.

The annual spring formal at the college had ended, and most of the students had left. A half-dozen faculty members were standing around the piano talking with the leader of the band. His name was Duke Ellington.

The conversation turned to religion and Ellington's recent sacred compositions. "Tell us about your version of Psalm 150," someone said. "Oh, yeah!" said the bandleader, and he called to one of the singers walking by, "Toney Watkins, come over here!"

Then they gave us their rendition of Psalm 150. Toney Watkins sang the words, and Duke

Ellington played the piano, filling in various instrumental parts with his own singing. "Praise the Lord with the sound of the trumpet," went the words, and Ellington said, "That where Cat Anderson takes a tremendous trumpet ride."

Years later I located a recording of that version of Psalm 150. The record jacket tells how the congregation in Barcelona, Spain, burst into the aisles of the ancient church of Santa Maria del Mar and started dancing when the Ellington band played Psalm 150 there. After all, the psalm says, "Praise him with tambourine and dance!"

The first psalm introduces the book of Psalms as a collection suited for meditation and identifies it as a prayer book. This last psalm suggests that the Psalms be accompanied by music and dancing. The book of Psalms is also a hymnbook or, to use the Hebrew title, a book of "Praises."

Praise. That is what the Psalms are all about. The German theologian Ludwig Koehler put it this way: "The deeper one descends through the centuries into the breadth of the Old Testament writings, the louder the praise and laud of God can be heard" (quoted in Westermann, *Praise and Lament* [see "For Further Reading"], 7). The book of Psalms has been put together as a handbook for praising God. It is divided into five "books," each of which ends with a psalm that concludes with a word of praise (Psalms 41, 72, 89, and 106). The fifth book ends with five psalms of praise, each of which is framed with "Hallelujah." With these psalms, the whole Psalter concludes with a mighty chorus of praises.

What is praise? Somewhere I heard a story about a small boy who wanted his mother to play darts with him. "Yes, I'll play," she said. Then she asked, "Shall we take turns? You throw, then I'll throw?" "No," said the boy, "I'll throw the darts. You just say, 'Wonderful!'" That is what praise is: Saying "Wonderful!" or "You're the greatest!" to another person. The Psalms suggest that saying "Wonderful!" or "How great thou art!" to God is one of the marks of the life of a believer.

This last of the psalms summarizes the *why,* the *how,* and the *who* of praising God. *Why* praise? "Praise him for his mighty deeds," says the psalm. That expression calls to mind what God has done, beginning with creation and continuing through setting Israel free from Egypt and setting those who believe in Jesus Christ free from sin, death, and the devil. For all of this, God is to be praised!

How should God be praised? That is the special concern of this final psalm. "Praise God with music, with dancing, and with enthusiasm!" it says.

Psalm 150 calls for all classes of musical instruments to be taken up in praise, including winds, strings, and percussion. To update it:

Praise him with trumpet and trombone,
    French horn and tuba;
  praise him with banjo and guitar, violin
    and viola!
Praise him with tambourine, castanets, and
    dancing;
  praise him with cello and bass viol,
  with clarinet, flute, and saxophone!
Praise him with the crash of cymbals,
  with crashing, clashing, $300 Zildjian
    cymbals!

Who should join this chorus, the orchestra of praises? Psalm 104 says that all living beings get their breath from the Lord (v. 29). Psalm 150 suggests that every living creature use that breath to join in praising God: "Let everything that breathes praise the LORD!"

King David knew something about praising God. When they brought into Jerusalem the portable altar that had accompanied Israel in the wilderness, the town band was out to meet them, and the king joined in the singing and dancing (2 Sam. 6:5, 14). The king was a musician himself, and many of the psalms are associated with him. Since David's time, these psalms have been used for praise by countless singers, dancers, trumpeters, and cymbal players.

This psalm invites all of God's creatures to find a place in the choir. It encourages all to join the chorus of those singing, playing, and dancing the praises of God.

The Response of Praise

The Hebrew title for the book of Psalms is "Praises." This suggests that while praise and lament run through the Psalms as twin themes, the dominant theme is praise. We have noted that the movement of the Psalter as a whole book is from lament to praise.

Narrative Praise or Thanksgiving

Claus Westermann has pointed out that the psalms of praise are of two fundamental types. First there are psalms that tell the story of a deliverance an individual or the community has experienced and that praise God for that specific act of deliverance. For example, an individual has been ill, has prayed for healing, and healing has come. That person wants to praise God and tell others about what God has done. Such praise is expressed in Psalm 30:

> I cried to you for help, O Lord my God,
>   and you healed me;
>   you kept me from the grave. . . .
> So I will not be silent;
>   I will sing praise to you. (30:2, 12 TEV)

These are also called individual psalms of thanksgiving. Other psalms in this category are 9; 18;

32; 40:1-11; 66:13-20; 92; 107; 116; 118; and 138.

Or it may happen that the community has won an important battle or escaped from an enemy. This, too, calls for praise:

Let us thank the LORD,
who has not let our enemies destroy us.
We have escaped like a bird from a hunter's
trap;
the trap is broken, and we are free!
(124:6-7 TEV)

Descriptive Praise or Hymns
The second type of psalm of praise is not occasioned by any specific event but simply praises God for who God is and for what God does. Because these psalms describe God, they are called psalms of descriptive praise, or hymns.

The structure of these hymns is simple. They begin with a call to praise in the imperative mood:

Praise the LORD!
You servants of the LORD, praise his name!
(113:1 TEV)

They continue with reasons for praise:

There is no one like the LORD our God.
He lives in the heights above,
but he bends down. . . . (113:5-6 TEV)

In some psalms, the reason for praising God is God's activity as Creator. These may be grouped together as the creation psalms, including 8; 19; 104; 139; and 148. In others, the reason for praising is God's actions in history. These may be considered together as historical psalms, including 78; 105; and 106; 135 and 136 praise God because of his action both as Creator and as director of history.

Certain psalms are so dominated by the imperative call to praise that little space is left for the reasons. This becomes increasingly the case with the quintet of "Hallelujah" psalms that conclude the Psalter.

The psalms of descriptive praise or hymns include 8; 19:1-6; 29; 33; 47; 65; 66:1-12; 89:1-37; 93; 95–100; 103; 104; 105; 111; 113–114; 117; 134; 136; 139; 145–150.

The World Is So Full of a Number of Things: Creation Psalms

O LORD, our Sovereign,
   how majestic is your name in all the earth!

You have set your glory above the heavens.
   Our of the mouths of babes and infants
you have founded a bulwark because of your
      foes,
   to silence the enemy and the avenger.

When I look at your heavens, the work of
      your fingers,
   the moon and the stars that you have
      established;
what are human beings that you are mind-
      ful of them,
   mortals that you care for them?

Yet you have made them a little lower than
      God,
   and crowned them with glory and honor.

You have given them dominion over the
     works of your hands;
  you have put all things under their feet,
all sheep and oxen,
     and also the beasts of the field,
the birds of the air, and the fish of the sea,
     whatever passes along the paths of the
     seas.

O LORD, our Sovereign,
  how majestic is your name in all the earth!
                    —Psalm 8

Midway between the Apes and the Angels (Psalm 8)

I listened to the astronomer as he lectured about the size of the universe. The blackboard was full of diagrams, and my head was full of facts. He spoke of spiral nebulae and black holes, of millions of light years and billions of galaxies. Then he suggested this model: Imagine that the sun is the size of a grapefruit. Then the earth would be the size of a grain of sand 35 feet away. The moon would be a tiny speck of sand an inch from the earth. Mercury would be 13 feet from the grapefruit; Venus, 25 feet; Mars, 53 feet. All these planets would be revolving around the grapefruit-sun.

The sun, he continued, is our closest star. On this scale, the next grapefruit-star would be 1,600 miles away, about the distance from Minneapolis to Los Angeles! To model our entire galaxy, we would need 10 billion grapefruit, each 1,600 miles apart. Our universe is made up of billions of such galaxies, all moving away from one another.

The classroom was getting stuffy, and I was getting a headache. Finally, the lecture ended. I walked home in the cool night air, from time to time looking up at the stars. I thought: The universe is very big. We humans are a very small part of it. Could it be that the Creator of all this pays any attention to us?

The writer of this psalm had been looking at the night sky. He addressed his thoughts to God:

> When I look at your heavens, the work of
>   your fingers,
>   the moon and the stars that you have
>   established;
> what are human beings that you are mind-
>   ful of them,
>   mortals that you care for them? (vv. 3-4)

The universe is very big, he thought. Human beings are a small part of it. Could it be that the Creator pays any attention to them? The psalm continues:

> Yet you have made them a little lower than
>   God,
>   and crowned them with glory and honor.

You have given them dominion over the
    works of your hands;
  you have put all things under their feet.
    (vv. 5-6)

Yes, says this psalm, the Creator does care, and in
fact has assigned us as human beings a position
just a little under God! We are called to be royalty, charged with managing the affairs of our
corner of the cosmos.

This psalm speaks *about* the cosmos, but it is
more interested in speaking *to* the Creator. The
psalm says something about astronomy, but it is
more interested in the astronomer. It can help all
of us—astronomers and farmers, housewives and
engineers—to find the place assigned to us in the
midst of the nebulae, the galaxies, and the creates
of this earth.

We humans are designed to be a "little less
than God" or, as the King James Version put it, "a
little lower than the angels." Of all the plant and
animal life on the earth, God invited us to share
the management task with him. This gives us
great dignity.

But these words also contain a warning. We
are intended to be *less* than God, *lower* than the
angels. This means that we ought not expect to
answer all questions, solve all mysteries, or con-
trol all aspects of our lives and the lives of others
on our planet. There are limits to our capabilities.
We ought not get ourselves confused with God,

or even with angels. The Bible labels such confusion the sin of pride.

We are also meant to be kings and queens, responsible for ruling over this planet. This means that our assignment is to care for the rivers and the forests, the whales and the whooping cranes, as well as for the orphans, the widows, and the poor. Such care is expected of royalty: the king "has pity on the weak and poor; he saved the lives of those in need" (Ps. 72:13 TEV).

Once I heard a biologist lecture about the nature of human life. The title of his speech was based on Psalm 8 in the King James Version: "Midway between the Apes and the Angels." This title helps us to remember who we are—not gods, nor even angels; but more than apes, or even dolphins. We are royalty, assigned to care for the earth, inviting our fellow earthlings to join in the chorus: "O LORD, our Sovereign, how majestic is your name!"

* * *

Praise the LORD, my soul!
   O LORD, my God, how great you are!
You are clothed with majesty and glory;
   you cover yourself with light.
You spread out the heavens like a tent
   and built your home on the waters above.
You use the clouds as your chariot
   and ride on the wings of the wind.

You use the winds as your messengers
  and flashes of lightning as your servants.

You have set the earth firmly on its founda-
    tions,
  and it will never be moved.
You placed the ocean over it like a robe,
  and the water covered the mountains.
When you rebuked the waters, they fled;
  they rushed away when they heard your
    shout of command.
They flowed over the mountains and into
    the valleys,
  to the place you had made for them.
You set a boundary they can never pass,
  to keep them from covering the earth
    again.

You make springs flow in the valleys,
  and rivers run between the hills.
They provide water for the wild animals;
  there the wild donkeys quench their thirst.
In the trees near by,
  the birds make their nests and sing.

From the sky you send rain on the hills,
  and the earth is filled with your blessings.
You make grass grow for the cattle
  and plants for man to use,

so that he can grow his crops
and produce wine to make him happy,
olive oil to make him cheerful,
and bread to give him strength.

The cedars of Lebanon get plenty of rain—
the LORD's own trees, which he planted.
There the birds build their nests;
the storks nest in the fir trees.
The wild goats live in the high mountains,
and the badgers hide in the cliffs.

You created the moon to mark the months;
the sun knows the time to set.
You made the night, and in the darkness
all the wild animals come out.
The young lions roar while they hunt,
looking for the food that God provides.
When the sun rises, they go back
and lie down in their dens.
Then people go out to do their work
and keep working until evening.

LORD, you have made so many things!
How wisely you made them all!
The earth is filled with your creatures.
There is the ocean, large and wide,
where countless creatures live,
large and small alike.

The ships sail on it, and in it plays Leviathan,
  that sea monster which you made.

All of them depend on you
  to give them food when they need it.
You give it to them, and they eat it;
  you provide food, and they are satisfied.
When you turn away, they are afraid;
  when you take away their breath, they die
  and go back to the dust from which they
    came.
But when you give them breath, they are
  created;
  you give new life to the earth.

May the glory of the LORD last forever!
  May the LORD be happy with what he has
    made!
He looks at the earth, and it trembles;
he touches the mountains, and they pour
  out smoke.

I will sing to the LORD all my life;
  as long as I live I will sing praises to my
    God.
May he be pleased with my song,
  for my gladness comes from him.
May sinners be destroyed from the earth;
  may the wicked be no more.

Praise the LORD, my soul!
Praise the LORD!

—Psalm 104 (TEV)

The World Is So Full of a Number of Things (Psalm 104)

It was a six-year-old boy who helped me to understand this psalm.

Those were the days when a backyard baseball game was an every evening occurrence at our house. The bat and the ball were made of plastic, but the intensity of each game was worthy of a World Series. I was the permanent pitcher and utility infielder. Our three sons rotated as batter, catcher, and all-purpose outfielder.

The moment was a crucial one. There was the pitch—swung on—a fly ball hit into deep center field! I turned to look, confident that our man in the outfield would handle it with ease. But he was not there. He was racing up the hill in pursuit of a monarch butterfly that had cruised past him. We left the bat and ball behind and spent the rest of the evening chasing butterflies.

That incident taught me something about wonder. Think of it: calling a baseball game on account of a butterfly! If that six-year-old had not been there, I would never have seen it go by.

Psalm 104 is an invitation to tour the wonderland where we live. It begins with a call to

"Praise the Lord" and continues with reasons for that praise.

The first reactions recall the creation, the psalmist speaking to God:

> You spread out the heavens like a tent
>> and built your home on the waters above.
> You use the clouds as your chariot
>> and ride on the wings of the wind. . . .
> You have set the earth firmly on its founda-
>> tions,
>> and it will never be moved.
> You placed the ocean over it like a robe
>> and the water covered the mountains.
>> (vv. 2-3, 5-6 TEV)

There are more reasons for praise. God continues to be involved in nature:

> You make springs flow in the valleys,
>> and rivers run between the hills.
> They provide water for the wild animals;
>> there the wild donkeys quench their thirst.
> In the trees near by,
>> the birds make their nests and sing.
>> (vv. 10-12 TEV)

God gives life to all creatures in this wonderland:

> All of them depend on you
>> to give them food when they need it. . . .
> When you take away their breath, they
>> die. (vv. 27, 29 TEV)

There is a kind of wonder that marvels at the spectacular. A rocket bursts in the night sky on the Fourth of July and the crowd chants, "Oooh!" But there is another kind of wonder that delights in the ordinary. This is wonder of a more mature sort, which marvels not only at the cardinal or the Baltimore oriole, but also at the robin and the sparrow.

Psalm 104 invites us to discover this ordinary kind of wonder in the world where we live. It points us to the cedar and the fir, the stork and the wild goat, the young lion and the badger. It calls our attention to the feel of the wind and the rain, the sight of a white cloud in the blue sky, the sound of a mourning dove's cooing, the smell of fresh bread, the taste of good wine.

This psalm encourages us to spend a lifetime marveling at the wonders that surround us, from the flight of the hummingbird to the song of the humpback whale, from the cry of a loon to the colors of yet another sunset.

We used to read to our children from a small book by Robert Louis Stevenson titled *A Child's Garden of Verses*. I don't remember any of the poems now. But I do recall the saying printed on the first page:

The world is so full of a number of things,
    I'm sure we should all be as happy as kings.

That's the way a six-year-old looks at the world. This psalm is an invitation to look at the world through the eyes of a child again. Notice that it does not stop with wonder at creation, but leads on to praise of the Creator. This tour of wonderland ends as it begins, with a call to "Praise the Lord!"

* * *

LORD, you have examined me and you know me.
You know everything I do;
   from far away you understand all my
      thoughts.
You see me, whether I am working or
   resting;
   you know all my actions.
Even before I speak,
   you already know what I will say.
You are all around me on every side;
   you protect me with your power.
Your knowledge of me is too deep;
   it is beyond my understanding.

Where could I go to escape from you?
   Where could I get away from your
      presence?
If I went up to heaven, you would be there;
   if I lay down in the world of the dead,
   you would be there.

If I flew away beyond the east
   or lived in the farthest place in the west,
   you would be there to lead me,
   you would be there to help me.
I could ask the darkness to hide me
   or the light around me to turn into night,
but even darkness is not dark for you,
   and the night is as bright as the day.
Darkness and light are the same to you.
You created every part of me;
   you put me together in my mother's
      womb.
I praise you because you are to be feared;
   all you do is strange and wonderful.
I know it with all my heart.
When my bones were being formed,
   carefully put together in my mother's
      womb,
when I was growing there in secret,
   you knew that I was there—
   you saw me before I was born.
The days allotted to me
   had all been recorded in your book,
   before any of them ever began.
O God, how difficult I find your thoughts;
   how many of them there are!
If I counted them, they would be more than
      the grains of sand.
   When I awake, I am still with you.

O God, how I wish you would kill the
   wicked!
   How I wish violent men would leave me
      alone!
They say wicked things about you;
   they speak evil things against your name.
O LORD, how I hate those who hate you!
   How I despise those who rebel against
      you!
I hate them with a total hatred;
   I regard them as my enemies.
Examine me, O God, and know my mind;
   test me, and discover my thoughts.
Find out if there is any evil in me
   and guide me in the everlasting way!
                              —Psalm 139 (TEV)

On Not Trying to Be Moses (Psalm 139)

I recall a college friend who had an unusual way
of spending the time before the beginning of a
concert or lecture. He was making a study of the
shape of people's ears. "All ears are different," he
told me one evening as he began to sketch the
basic types in the margin of the program. There
are ears that turn out and ears that turn in. There
is the rare, but always fascinating, ear with the
fused lobe.

Then he continued, "Not only are all ears different, but no two ears on the same head are
exactly alike." Sure enough. Careful observation

supported his contention. One could detect a distinctive twist in one, a subtle turn in the other.

The point is this: Everyone is different. That's the way God makes things. Think of leaves. Or snowflakes. Or ears.

Psalm 139 may be considered a creation psalm. It does not speak of God creating the whole universe. This one is between the psalmist and God:

> You created every part of me;
>> you knit me together in my mother's womb. (v. 13 TEV, alt.)

This is a most unusual picture: God the knitter! My mother-in-law has knitted Norwegian sweaters for each of the six members of our family. They are beautiful and warm, able to keep out both the cold and the rain. I watched as she knitted those sweaters. The process is very complicated—keeping the pattern straight, getting the design just right.

"You knit me together," says this psalm. It is complicated to knit a Norwegian sweater. But it is much more complicated to knit a Norwegian! Or an African, or an American. The psalmist thinks about that and says to God:

> I praise you, because you are to be feared;
>> all you do is strange and wonderful.
> I know it with all my heart. (v. 14 TEV)

God "created every part of me." This psalm gives you a certain dignity. As you look at others, you may feel that you are not worth very much. Others are better looking, smarter, richer, or have a nicer family. But this psalm says: Wait a minute! For some reason, God put together that combination of genes and chromosomes, eyes and ears, that turned out to be you:

> [You saw my bones] being formed,
>> carefully put together in my mother's womb,
> when I was growing there in secret. . . .
> You saw me before I was born.
> The days that had been created for me
>> had all been recorded in your book,
>> before any of them ever began.
> (vv. 15-16 TEV)

Once I heard a story about a young rabbi named Zusia. He was discouraged about his work. He would preach and his congregation would look out the window or doze off. The young people thought he was old-fashioned. He was not making an impact on the community. He knew he wasn't much of a scholar. He saw himself as a failure.

So Zusia visited an older rabbi and said, "Rabbi, I'm so discouraged. What can I do?"

The old rabbi said, "My son, when you get to heaven, God is not going to say to you, 'Why weren't you Moses?' But he is going to ask, 'Why weren't you Zusia?' So why don't you stop trying to be Moses, and just be the Zusia that God made you to be?"

I remember putting our three boys to bed when they were small. For some reason, one of them had an unusual twist to his evening prayers. He would go through the list like his brothers, "Thank you for my mom and dad, thank you for my dog, thank you for my brothers and sister. . . ." But then, quite matter-of-factly, he added his own touch, "Thank you for me."

This psalm calls each of us to go through life being the person God made us to be and then to join the psalmist in saying, "I praise you because you are to be feared; all you do is strange and wonderful" (v. 14 TEV).

For Further Reading

The Psalms

The HarperCollins Study Bible: New Revised Standard Version with the Apocryphal/Deuterocanonical books. Wayne A. Meeks, general editor. New York: HarperCollins, 1993. Especially valuable are the introduction and comments on the Psalms by Patrick D. Miller.

Commentaries

Kraus, Hans-Joachim. *Psalms 1–59* and *Psalms 60–150.* Translated by H. C. Oswald. Minneapolis: Augsburg, 1988, 1989. Masterful introduction and exposition; a definitive work.

Limburg, James. *Psalms.* Westminster Bible Companion. Louisville: Westminster John Knox, 2000. Intends to show the meaning of the psalms for our time; written for lay people.

Luther, Martin. *Selected Psalms I, II, III.* Vols. 12–14 of *Luther's Works,* edited by Jaroslav Pelikan. St. Louis: Concordia, 1955, 1956, 1958. Always interesting and insightful interpretations.

Mays, James L. *Psalms*. Interpretation: A Bible Commentary for Teaching and Preaching. Louisville: Westminster John Knox, 1994. A classic, especially for teachers and preachers.

McCann, J. Clinton, Jr. *The Book of Psalms*. Vol. 4 of *The New Interpreter's Bible*. Nashville: Abingdon, 1996. Fine exposition, always pointing out the relevance of the psalm for the present time.

Other Works

Brueggemann, Walter. *Spirituality of the Psalms*. Facets. Minneapolis: Fortress, 2001. Examines the types and themes of the Psalms in a brief, readable format.

Holladay, William L. *The Psalms through Three Thousand Years: Prayerbook of a Cloud of Witnesses*. Minneapolis: Fortress, 1993. Fascinating story of the interpretation of the Psalms.

Limburg, James. "Psalms, Book of." In *The Anchor Bible Dictionary*, vol. 5. Edited by David Noel Freedman. New York: Doubleday, 1992. Basic information on the Psalms, including Dead Sea Scrolls, Hebrew poetry, psalm types, etc.

Mays, James L. *The Lord Reigns: A Theological Handbook to the Psalms*. Louisville: Westminster John Knox, 1994. Essays of fundamental importance for psalm interpretation.

Miller, Patrick D. *Interpreting the Psalms*. Philadelphia: Fortress, 1986. Helpful essays and model expositions of selected psalms.

———. *They Cried to the Lord: The Form and Theology of Biblical Prayer.* Minneapolis: Fortress, 1994. Basic information on prayer and lament in the Psalms.

Westermann, Claus. *The Living Psalms.* Translated by J. R. Porter. Grand Rapids: Eerdmans, 1989.

———. *Praise and Lament in the Psalms.* Translated by Keith R. Crim and Richard N. Soulen. Atlanta: John Knox, 1981.

———. *The Psalms: Structure, Content, and Message.* Translated by Ralph D. Gehrke. Minneapolis: Augsburg, 1980. These three books provide an introduction to the author's brilliant studies of the Psalms.

Acknowledgments

Scripture quotations, unless otherwise noted, are from the New Revised Standard Version Bible, copyright © 1989 by the Division of Christian Education of the National Council of the Churches of Christ in the USA, and are used by permission.

Scripture quotations marked TEV are from the Good News Bible, Today's English Version, copyright © 1966, 1971, 1976 by American Bible Society. Used by permission.

Scripture quotations marked RSV are from the Revised Standard Version of the Bible, copyright © 1946, 1952, 1971 by the Division of Christian Education of the National Council of the Churches of Christ in the USA, and are used by permission.

The quotation from *Jesus Christ Superstar* in Chapter 2 is from "I Only Want to Say (Gethsemane)," lyrics by Tim Rice, music by Andrew Lloyd Webber, © 1970 by MCA Music Ltd., London, England. Sole selling agent Leeds Music Corporation (MCA), New York, N.Y., for North, South and Central America. Used by permission. All rights reserved.